14

VIKAS LIBRARY OF MODERN INDIAN WRITING

MODERN INDIAN FICTION

MODERN INDIAN FICTION

Edited by

SAROS COWASJEE
Professor of English
University of Regina, Regina (Canada)

VASANT A. SHAHANE
Professor of English
Osmania University, Hyderabad (India)

VIKAS PUBLISHING HOUSE PVT LTD

VIKAS PUBLISHING HOUSE PVT LTD
Regd. Office: 5 Ansari Road, New Delhi 110002
H.O.: VIKAS HOUSE, 20/4 Industrial Area,
Sahibabad, Distt. Ghaziabad, U.P. (India).

COPYRIGHT © SAROS COWASJEE and VASANT A. SHAHANE, 1981

1V2C4801

ISBN 0-7069-1051-6

Printed at India Printers, Esplanade Road, Delhi 110006

PREFACE

Yet another anthology! Yes, but with a difference. This is the only anthology of its kind to offer to readers in India and abroad a selection from novels written by Indians in English. It includes eight episodes, more or less self-contained, from the works of eight novelists who have made their mark in fiction. Four of these novelists are also accomplished short-story writers, and a short story of each has also been included.

This anthology is designed primarily for the student and the general reader who, despite his interest in Indian literature, is not sure where to begin and what authors to read. Which of an author's dozen novels should be read first? And would not a wrong choice hinder him from further exploring the works of the same author? The selection we offer here is not necessarily representative of an author's work, but it is taken from one of his more significant works and throws light on his art, style and treatment of Indian life. Even a cursory glance at the volume shows the diversity and range of Indian fiction. At one end of the scale we have Mulk Raj Anand whose writings are marked by an unrelenting concern for the poor, and who frrely interjects Hindi words into English and makes literal translations of Indian idiom into English to convey Indian feeling and nuances. At the other end of the scale we have novelists like R.K. Narayan and Kamala Markandaya who refuse to take liberties with the English language and write in impeccable prose.

Whether a writer is forging a new language for expressing or using standard English, his subject is always India—modern

India with all its contradictions and complexity. This slim volume offers, more than any compendium of Indian fiction, some of the best writings by Indians in English.

Each episode in this anthology is preceded by a bio-bibliographical note and a plot outline of the novel from which the episode is selected. An attempt has also been made to incorporate some pertinent criticism of the authors and to place the episodes in their proper context. There is also a glossary of Indian words which appear in the text and which foreign readers should find particularly useful. Unlike, as in most anthologies, no questions are put to test the readers' comprehension—the general reader has little use for them, and the university student and teacher are perceptive enough to formulate the right questions themselves and need no help from us.

SAROS COWASJEE
VASANT A. SHAHANE

CONTENTS

	Preface	v
1.	**MULK RAJ ANAND**	1
	Coolie	2
	Duty	14
2.	**BHABANI BHATTACHARYA**	21
	He Who Rides A Tiger	22
	Steel Hawk	36
3.	**RUTH PRAWER JHABVALA**	43
	A Backward Place	45
4.	**MANOHAR MALGONKAR**	70
	The Princes	72
	The Fixer	96
5.	**KAMALA MARKANDAYA**	104
	The Nowhere Man	105
6.	**R. K. NARAYAN**	115
	The Guide	117
	Leela's Friend	130
7.	**RAJA RAO**	137
	Kanthapura	139
	The Cow of the Barricades	156

Contents

8. **KHUSHWANT SINGH** — 163
   - TRAIN TO PAKISTAN — 165
   - KARMA — 185

   GLOSSARY — 193

1. MULK RAJ ANAND

Born of Kshatriya parents in Peshawar in 1905, Mulk Raj Anand was educated at the Universities of Punjab and London. After earning his Ph.D. in 1929 on 'The Treatment of Relations by Locke and Hume,' he began writing notes for T.S.Eliot's *Criterion* and came to know such eminent writers as E.M. Forster, Herbert Read, Henry Miller and George Orwell. After a struggle of five years, he made his reputation with his first two novels: *Untouchable* (1935) and *Coolie* (1936). He followed up his success with *Two Leaves and a Bud* (1937) and the well-known trilogy *The Village* (1939), *Across the Black Waters* (1940) and *The Sword and the Sickle* (1942). By the time Anand returned to India in 1945, there were many who regarded him as the most distinguished Indian novelist writing in English. His works had received wide notice, and he himself was being hailed as the first writer to have dispelled the myth built around the stereotype Indian character: the myth about 'contentment' in the midst of poverty, 'mystical silences,': 'spiritual attainments.' In his novels, for the first time, the Indian masses had been clearly and intimately described with pitiless realism and deep understanding, and the exploiters—whether imperialists or feudalists—fiercely denounced.

Since 1946 Anand has made Bombay his home and centre of activity. It was here he wrote *Private Life of an Indian Prince* (1953), which is undoubtedly his finest literary achievement. He edits the art magazine *Marg*, and takes a keen interest in India's literary and cultural life. Writing is still his main preoccupation (he is the author of over forty books) and he is presently working on a monumental autobiographical novel in seven volumes called *The Seven Ages of Man*. Of these, three have so far been published.

Coolie is a study in destitution. It relates a series of adventures in the picaresque manner, except that the hero is no rogue but himself a victim of the world's rogueries. Munoo, a hillboy, is forced to leave his idyllic village in the Kangra valley so that he may earn a living and see the world. The first contact with reality shatters his dreams. Arriving at the house of a bank clerk, he falls foul of a shrewish and vindictive housewife, and before he flees from his employers' frenzied rage he has relieved himself near their doorstep and thereby lowered their social prestige.

He next finds himself at a primitive pickle and jam factory, hidden away among the reeking dark alleys of a feudal town. The proprietor who has befriended him is bankrupted by the thievery of his partner, and Munoo is on the street again. He arrives in Bombay and attaches himself to a vagrant family and becomes one of the workers in a cotton mill. He sweats to earn his bread in appalling working conditions. He makes new friends, has his first glimpse of life in a red-light district, and witnesses a Hindu-Muslim feud. Finally, he is knocked down by the car of an Anglo-Indian woman who takes him to Simla as her servant. In Simla he contacts tuberculosis (which is aggravated by his having to pull a rickshaw for his mistress), and dies watching the peaceful hills and valleys he had abandoned for the plains.

The following episode comes early in the novel, soon after Munoo has been installed as a servant in the household of Babu Nathoo Ram:

Coolie

Unfortunately, however, the road to perfection is punctuated by pitfalls, and it was not long before he tripped up and brought the odium of his mistress's wrath upon himself.

It so happened that Mr W.P. England came to tea with Babu Nathoo Ram and family one afternoon.

Mr England was the chief cashier of the Sham Nagar branch of the Imperial Bank of India in whose office Babu Nathoo Ram was a sub-accountant. He was a tall Englishman with an awkward, shuffling gait accentuated by the wooden, angular shape of his feet marching always hesitantly at an angle of forty-five degrees, and with a small, lined, expressionless face, only defined by the thick glasses on his narrow, myopic eyes. He had a rather good-natured smile on his thin lips, and it was that which led to the tea-party.

Babu Nathoo Ram had seen this smile play upon Mr England's lips every morning when the Sahib said 'Good morning' to him in response to his salute. There seemed little doubt that it was a kind smile which betokened the kindness of Mr England's heart, exactly as the frown on the face of Robert Horne, Esq., Manager of the Imperial Bank of India, Sham Nagar, betokened a vicious temperament. But then Mr England spoke so few words. The smile might just be a patronising, put-on affair. And it was very important to Babu Nathoo Ram's purpose to know whether it was a genuine smile or an assumed one. For he wanted a recommendation from Mr England to support his application for an increase in salary and promotion to the position of the Accountant. He had aspired to this position for a long time now, but he had not been able to attain it because Babu Afzul-ul-Haq occupied it, as he had occupied it for the last twenty years.

Mr England was a new officer. The Babu wanted to get him to write a recommendation before he was influenced by all the other English Officers in the Club and began to hate all Indians, before the kind smile on his lips became a smile of contempt and derision, or before it became sardonic on account of the weather. So he did not wait till he got to know Mr England better, or till Mr England got to know his work a little more, but he asked him to tea.

It had taken a great deal of courage, of course, and a lot more effort for him to ask Mr England to tea.

At first he had tried several mornings to muster enough courage to say something beyond the usual 'Good morning. Sir.' There seemed to be nothing to make the basis for an exchange of words, not even a file or letter, because they met on arrival at the office before the mail was opened. And later in the day, there was much too much to say about files for an informal exchange of ideas. Babu Nathoo Ram began to contemplate Mr England's ever-ready smile with a certain exasperation. And he believed more than ever that these Englishmen were very slippery and confounding because they were so reticent, just gaping at you without talking and without letting you talk.

Then someone (it was a barrister friend of Nathoo Ram) told him that, from his experience in England, he had found that the only way of starting a conversation with an Englishman was by talking to him about the weather.

'Good morning, Sir,' said Babu Nathoo Ram respectfully every morning, without daring to use the new knowledge.

'Good morning,' mumbled England, always smiling his nice smile, but rather self-conscious, because he saw that the Babu was older than he by at least twenty years, and his reverence seemed rather out of place. Besides, the Babu was a rich man. He had forty thousand rupees' worth of shares in the Allahabad Bank and was surely a trusted ally of the Government, which owned most of the Banks. He certainly was highly thought of and honored by the English directors of most of the Banks. But why did he not live up to his status? Horne was right, he reflected, when he said that these Indians were embarrassingly obsequious. He did not ask, however, why they were obsequious.

Nathoo Ram walked sheepishly behind Mr England in the hall one day, and the Sahib was rather ill at ease as he stepped angularly along in the cool shade cast by the drawn blinds on the windows.

'Fine morning, Sir! Beautiful day!' announced Nathoo Ram suddenly.

Mr England shuffled his feet, hesitated and turned round as if a thunderbolt had struck him. His face was suddenly pale with peevishness. Then he controlled himself and, smiling a sardonic smile, said:

'Yes, of course, very fine! Very beautiful!'

The Babu did not understand the sarcasm implicit in the Sahib's response. He was mightily pleased with himself that he had broken the ice, although he could not muster the courage to say anything more and ask him to tea.

That he did after sitting in the office for whole days, waiting in suspense for the right moment to come. It came when England, seeking to relieve the tension and to put Nathoo Ram at ease, approached the Babu's table one day before going off to lunch.

'How are you, Nathoo Ram?' he said.

'Fine morning, Sir,' said Nathoo Ram, suddenly looking up from the ledger and springing to attention as he balanced his pen, babu-like, across his ear.

'Yes, a bit too fine for my taste,' replied England.

'Yes, Sir,' said Nathoo Ram, wondering what to say.

There was an awkward pause in which England looked at the Babu and the Babu looked at England.

'Well, I am going off to lunch,' said the Sahib, 'though I can't eat much in this heat.'

'Sir,' said the Babu, jumping at his chance, 'you must eat Indian food. It's very tasty.' He couldn't utter the words fast enough.

'The Khansamah at the Club cooks curry sometimes,' returned England. 'I don't like it very much, it is too hot.'

'Sir, my wife cooks very good curries. You must come and taste one of our dishes,' ventured Nathoo Ram, tumbling over his words.

'No, I don't like curries,' said England. 'Thank you very much all the same.' And smiling his charming smile, he made to go. He had realised that he was becoming too familiar with the native, a thing his friends at the Club had warned him about.

'Will you come to see my house one day, Sir?' called Nathoo Ram eagerly and with beating heart. 'My wife would be honored if you would condescend to favour us with the presence of your company at tea, Sir. My brother, Sir——'

England had almost moved his head in negation, but he ducked it to drown his confusion.

'Yes, Sir, yes, Sir, today.'

'No,' said England. 'No, perhaps some day.'

After that Nathoo Ram had positively pestered England with his invitations to tea. Every time he met him, morning, noon, afternoon, he requested the favour of Mr England's gracious and benign condescension at tea.

At last England agreed to come, one day, a week hence.

For a week preparations for this party went on in the Babu's household, and Munoo had more than his share of the excitement. The carpets were lifted and dusted, and, though all the paraphernalia of the Babu's household, pictures, bottles, books, utensils and children's toys and clothes, lay in their original confusion, a rag was passed over everything to make it neat and respectable.

The news of a Sahib's projected visit to the Babu Nathoo Ram's house had spread all round the town, and in the neighboring houses, dirty, sackcloth curtains were hung up to guard female decorum from the intrusion of foreign eyes.

As Mr England walked up, stupidly dressed for the occasion in a warm navy-blue suit, with Nathoo Ram on the one side and Prem Chand, the Babu's doctor brother, on the other, and with Daya Ram, the chaprasi, in full regalia following behind, he felt hot and bothered.

Between mopping his brow with a large silk handkerchief and blushing at the Babu's reiterated gratitude and flattery, England wondered what Nathoo Ram's house was going to be like. Would it be like his father's home in Brixton, a semi-detached house on the Hay Mill estate, which they had furnished on the hire-purchase system with the help of Mr Drage and where he had occupied the maid's room when he was a clerk in the Midland Bank, before he came here and suddenly became a chief cashier? Or would it be like the house of 'Abdul Kerim, the Hindoo,' in that Hollywood film called *The Swami's Curse*, with fountains in the hall, around which danced the various wives of the Babu in clinging draperies and glittering ornaments?

The outlook of the flat-roofed hovels jutting into each other on the uprise to which the Babu pointed was rather disconcerting.

"Sahib! Sahib!' a cry went up, and there was a noise of several people rushing behind sackcloth curtains.

'The Mohammedans keep strict purdah, Sir,' informed Babu Nathoo Ram. 'And it is the women of the household of Babu Afzul-ul-Haq running to hide themselves.' 'Fate is favourable.' the Babu thought, for he had been able to have a dig at his Mussalman adversary.

Mr England smiled in a troubled manner as he looked aside.

'Look out!' Dr Prem Chand called. 'Your head!'

Mr England just missed hitting his forehead against the narrow doorway which led beyond the small veranda into the Babu's sitting-room. The pink of his face heightened to purple.

There was hardly any room to stand or to walk in the low-ceilinged, six foot by ten room, especially as both Nathoo Ram and Daya Ram had rushed to get a chair ready for the Sahib to sit upon.

Mr England stood looking round at the junk. He felt as tall as Nelson's column in this crowded atmosphere.

He could not see much, but as he sank into a throne-like chair he faced the clay image of the elephant god, Genesha garlanded with a chain of faded flowers. He thought it a sinister image, something horrible, one of the heathen idols which he had been taught to hate in the Wesleyan chapel he had attended with his mother.

'The god of wisdom, worldliness and wealth, Sir,' said Babu Nathoo Ram, defining his words rather pompously, as he knew his illiterate wife was overhearing him talk English to a Sahib, on an equal footing, for once in his life.

'Interesting,' mumbled Mr England.

'I hope to go to England for higher studies, Mr England,' said Dr Prem Chand, more at ease because he was an independent practitioner of medicine and not the Sahib's subordinate like his elder brother.

'Yes, really!' remarked England, brightening at the suggestion of 'home,' as all Englishmen in India learn to do.

'I suppose you have a big residence there,' asked Prem Chand, 'and perhaps you could give me some advice about my courses of study.'

'Yes,' said England in reply, blushing to realize that though he had to pose as a big top to these natives, he had no home to speak of, the semi-detached house in Brixton being not yet paid for, and he remembered that he had never been to a university and knew nothing about 'courses of study,' except those of Pitman's Typewriting and Shorthand School in Southampton Row, which he had attended for a season before going to the Midland Bank. He felt he should make a clean breast of it all, as he was really extremely honest. But his compatriots at the Club had always exhorted him to show himself off as the son of King George himself if need be. A guilty conscience added its weight of misery to his embarrassment.

'This is a family photograph taken on the occasion of my marriage, Sir,' said Nathoo Ram, lifting a huge, heavily-framed picture off its peg and clumsily dropping two others, so that Munoo, who stood in the doorway, staring at the rare sight of the pink man, rushed in to save them.

Mr England looked up with a face not devoid of curiosity.

The Babu brought the picture along and, half apprehensive of the liberties he was taking, planted it on the Sahib's knees. Mr England held it at the sides and strained his eyes almost on to the glass to scrutinize it.

Munoo was drawn by the instinctive desire for contact, which knows no barriers between high and low, to come and stand almost at the sahib's elbow and join in the contemplation of the picture.

'Go away, you fool,' whispered the Babu and nudged the boy with his sharp, bony elbow.

Mr England, who was almost settling down, was disturbed.

He did not know who Munoo was, but he might be the Babu's son. If so, it was cruel for Nathoo Ram to drive him away like that, though he was glad that the dirtily clad urchin had not come sniffling up to him, for he might be carrying some disease of the skin. All these natives, Horne said, were disease-ridden. And from the number of lepers in the street, he seemed to be right.

'The servant boy,' said Nathoo Ram confidently to the Sahib in a contemptuous tone, to justify his rudeness to Munoo.

The Sahib assented by twisting his lips and screwing his eyes into an expression of disgust.

'This is my wife, Sir,' said Nathoo Ram, pointing to a form loaded with clothes and jewelry, which sat in the middle of the group, dangling its legs in a chair and with its face entirely covered by a double veil.

Mr England looked eagerly to scan the face in the picture and, not being able to see it, blamed his myopic eyes, as he pretended to appreciate the charm of the Babu's wife by saying, 'Nice-very nice.'

But lifting his hand he saw that it was covered with dust, which lay thickly on the back of the frame, and that his trousers were ruined. He frowned.

'My wife does not observe purdah, but she is very shy,' said the Babu apologetically. 'So she will not come in as is the custom with the women of your country.' In the same breath he switched on again to the picture: 'This is my humble self as the bridegroom, when I was young.'

Mr England saw the form of a heavily turbaned, feebler incarnation of Nathoo Ram, with rings in his ears, garlands round his neck and white English-Indian clothes, as he stood stiffly caressing the arm of his bride's chair with the left hand and showing a European watch to the world with the right.

Mr England's eyes scanned the wizened forms of dark men in the background of the picture. They then rested on two boys, who lay, reclining their heads against each other and on their elbows, in the manner of the odd members of cricket teams in Victorian photographs.

'Ain-ain—wain—ain—ain—ai—an,' a throaty wail wound its way out of the trumpet of the gramophone which Dr Prem Chand had set in motion.

Munoo rushed up to the door, really to hear the voice from the box sing, but making an excuse of the message that tea was ready. Sheila, who had just returned from school, came in too.

'This is our Indian music, Sir,' said Nathoo Ram proudly; 'a ghazal, sung by Miss Janki Bai of Allahabad. 'My elder daughter,' he added, pointing to Sheila. Then turning to her he said, 'Come and meet the Sahib.'

The child was shy and stood obstinately in the doorway, smiling awkwardly.

Mr England's confusion knew no bounds. He was perspiring profusely. The noise and commotion created by the 'ain—ain—wai—ain' were unbearable. His ears were used at the best to the exotic zigzag of Charleston or Rumba or his native tunes 'Love Is Like a Cigarette,' 'Rosemarie, I Love You' and 'I want to be Happy, but I can't be Happy till I make You Happy too.' And he felt the children staring at him.

He wished it would all be over soon. He regretted that he had let himself in for it all.

'Go and get the tea,' said Nathoo Ram to Munoo.

'Yes, Babuji,' said Munoo as he ran back, excited and happy.

He nearly knocked into his uncle Daya Ram, who was coming towards the sitting-room bearing heaps of syrupy, Indian sweets and hot maize flour dumplings which Bibiji had been frying in a deep pan of olive oil the whole afternoon.

Bibiji saw Munoo rushing and would have abused him, but she was on her best behavior today. Only she gave him a furious look as she pushed some dishes of English pastries from outside the four lines of her kitchen, commanding him to take them to the sitting-room.

Munoo was in high spirits, far too exalted by the pleasure of the Sahib's company in his master's house to be damped by Bibiji's frowns. He took the dishes over, his mouth watering at the sight of the sweets.

He placed the pastries on the huge writing table which had been converted for use as a dinner-table. He waited to look at the Sahib. A scowl on the Babu's face sent him back to the kitchen to fetch the tea-tray.

Meanwhile Babu Nathoo Ram had began to offer food to the Sahib.

The Babu took up two dishes in his hands and brought them up to Mr England's nose.

'Sir, this is our famous sweetmeat, gulabjaman by name,' he said, 'and this is called by the name of rasgula. Made from fresh cream, Sir. The aroma of the attar of roses has been cast over them. They were specially made to my order by the confectioner.'

The perfume of the rasgulas and gulabjamans as well as the sight of them made Mr. England positively sick. He recoiled from the attack of the syrupy stuff on his senses with a murmur of 'No, thank you.'

'Oh yes, Sir, yes, Sir,' urged Babu Nathoo Ram.

If Mr England had been offered a plate and a fork, or a spoon, he might have taken one of the sweets. But he was supposed to pick them up with his hand. That was impossible to the Englishman, who had never picked up even a chicken-bone in his fingers to do full justice to it.

'Some pakoras, then?' said the Babu. 'They are a specialty of my wife. Come, Daya Ram.'

The peon brought up the dish of the maize--flour-dumplings. The sharp smell of the oily dark-brown stuff was enough to turn Mr England's liver. He looked at it as if it were poison and said, 'No, no, thank you, really, I had a late luncheon.'

'Well, if you don't care for Indian sweets, Sir,' said Nathoo Ram in a hurt voice, 'then please eat English-made pastry that I specially ordered from Stiffles. You must, Sir.,'

The pastries, too, were thickly coated with sugar and looked forbidding.

'No, thanks, really. I can't eat in this hot weather,' said England, trying to give a plausible excuse.

Now Nathoo Ram was disappointed. If the Sahib did not eat and did not become indebted to him, how could he ever get the recommendation he needed?

'Sir, Sir,' he protested, thrusting the food again under England's nose. 'Do please eat something—just a little bit of a thing.'

'No, thank you very much, Nathoo Ram. Really,' said England, 'I will take a cup of tea and then I must go. I am a very busy man, you know.

'Sir,' said Nathoo Ram, his under-lip quivering with emotion, 'I had hoped that you would partake of the simple hospitality that I, your humble servant, can extend to you. But you will have tea, tea... Tea. Oh! Munoo, bring the tea!"

Munoo was hurrying in with the tea-tray. When he heard his master's call he scurried. The tea-tray fell from his hands. All the china lay scattered on the kitchen floor.

Mr England heard the crash and guessed that a disaster had taken place.

Babu Nathoo Ram's heart sank. He had spent five rupees of his well-earned money on the tea-party. And it had all gone to waste.

Dr Prem Chand walked deliberately out into the kitchen and cowed Bibiji into a forced restraint, poured the remains of tea and milk into a cup and brought it on a neat saucer, saying coolly, with a facetious smile:

'Our servant, Munoo, Mr England, knows that a Japanese tea-set only costs one rupee twelve annas. So he does not care how many cups and saucers he breaks.'

Mr England was sweating with the heat. He became pale with embarrassment and fury. His small mouth contracted. He took the cup of tea and sipped it. It was hot, it almost scalded his lips and tongue.

'I must go now,' he said, and rose from his eminent position on the throne-like chair.

'We are disappointed, Sir,' said Nathoo Ram, apologizing and humble. 'But I and my wife hope you will come again.' And he followed the Sahib sheepishly, as England veered round suddenly and shuffled out on his awkward feet.

'Look out! Your head!' said Dr Prem Chand warning the Sahib in time before he was again likely to hit the low doorway, 'Good afternoon.'

Mr England smiled, then assumed a stern expression and walked out silently, followed by Babu Nathoo Ram and Daya Ram, past groups of inquisitive men and children.

The tea-party had been a fiasco.

Dr Prem Chand went into the kitchen. He was going to enjoy the sweets. But his sister-in-law was shouting at Munoo.

'Vay, may you die, may you be broken, may you fade away, you blind one! Do you know what you have done? May the flesh of your dead body rot in hell! With what evil star did you come to this house, that you do everything wrong? That china cost us almost as much money as you earn in a month.'

'That Englishman has no taste,' said Prem Chand, coming in; 'he did not eat a thing.'

'It is all the fault of this eater of his masters,' she cried, pointing to Munoo, 'May he die!'

'How is he responsible for that monkey-faced man's bad taste?' asked Prem Chand, 'and how is he to be blamed for all this junk in your house which apparently annoyed the Sahib?'

'Don't you encourage this dead one, Prem!' said Bibiji. 'Our house used to be like the houses of the Sahiblogs until this brute came from the hills and spoilt it all. That lovely set of china he has broken, the uncivilized brute!'

'Well now, you get a pair of sun-glasses gratis for every four annas' worth of Japanese goods that you buy in the bazaar,' mocked Prem, 'so we will all have eye-glasses, even you, Bibiji!'

Munoo did not know whether to laugh or to cry. A shock of apprehension had passed through him when he dropped the china, and seized his soul in a knot of fear. He stood dumb. The mockery of the chota Babu stirred the warmth on the surface of his blood. He awakened from his torpor and smiled.

Bibiji sprang from her seat near the kitchen and gave him a sharp, clean slap on the cheek.

'You spoiler of our salt!' she raved. 'You have brought bad luck to our house! You beast! And I have tried hard to correct you—'

'Oh, leave him alone,' said Prem. 'It is not his fault.' And he went towards the boy.

'Don't let me hear you wail, or I will kill you, you stupid fool!' said Babu Nathoo Ram angrily as he came in with tear-filled eyes.

It was not the first time that Munoo succumbed to sleep, stifling his sobs and his cries.

Duty

THE midday sun blasts everything in the Indian summer: it scorches the earth till its upper layers crack into a million fissures; it sets fire to the water till the lakes and pools and swamps bubble, evaporate and dry up; it shrivels up the lives of birds, beasts and flowers; it burns into one like red pepper and leaves one gasping for breath with a bulging tongue till one spends one's time looking for some shady spot for even the most precarious shelter.

Mangal Singh, the policeman who had been posted on duty

at the point where the branch road from the village of Vadala enters the Mall Road of Chetpur, had taken shelter under the sparse foliage of a kikar tree beyond the layers of white dust, after having stood in the sun for five and a half hours since dawn. In a little while sepoy Rahmat-Ullah would come and relieve him, and he felt that he could cool down a little and prepare to go to the barracks.

The sun was penetrating even the leaves of the wayside trees, and there was not much comfort in the humid airless atmosphere, but after the cracking heat of the open, Mangal felt that this comparative shade was a blessing.

He was not, of course, like the delicate Lallas, rich Hindu merchants, who rode out into the gardens early in the morning and withdrew after 'eating' the fresh air at sunrise and never appeared till sunset, sitting in the laps of their wives drinking milk-water or lying sprawled about on the front boards of their shops under the cool air of electric fans. . . . 'No he didn't say as they would: 'I go for a pice worth of salt, bring me a palanquin.' Nor could he quench his thirst by drinking dew.' No, he was proud that he came from strong peasant stock and was a hardy policeman who could rough it: indeed, this police service was not active enough for him and he felt it a pity that he had not become a real sepoy; for there was more pay in the paltans and there were better uniforms, also free mufti and free rations. So he had heard after he had put the mark of his thumb down and joined the police force—but once done cannot be undone. And it was the blessing of the Gurus, as there was little chance of earning any extra money in the military; while, apart from the fifteen rupees pay, there were other small sums so long as confectioners continued to mix milk with water and so long as there was a murder or two in the prostitutes' bazaar, and so long as there were respectable Lallas who would pay rather than have their names mentioned. . . .Why, even here on point duty in the waste land—' your own is your own and another's is also yours.' For if the peasants offered tokens of grain and butter and sugar to the Munshi at the customs house, then why not to the police? That skinny little Babu at the octroi post had not the strong arm of the sepoy to protect them when they were being looted by the thugs in the market. . . . He knew. After wisdom the club. If only he had been able to pay a nazar to the Tehsildar he would never have lost his land to Seth Jhinda Ram. . . . But God's work was well done, man's badly. And, truly, if he had not pressed the limbs of the landlord the would never have got the recommendation to join the police. And you learnt a great deal in the service of the Sarkar. And there was nothing better than service: no worry, and there was so much at in it that these very cowardly city folk who laughed at you if you were a peasant joined their hands in obeisance to you if you wielded a truncheon. And the rustics who had no notion of discipline or duty could be made to obey authority with the might of the stave, and if they didn't obey that, the fear of the handcuff—even a daring robber like Barkat Ali could not escape because one could blow the whistle and call the entire police force out. And the Sarkar is truly powerful. Like Alamgir, it leaves no fire in the hearth, nor water in the jar, to bring a man to justice. . . .

He glanced at his dust-covered feet in the regulation shoes of rough cow-hide, even as he congratulated himself on his lucky position as a member of the much-feared police service and wished he had really been in the army, for there the sepoys had boots given them. His puttees too were old and faded and there was something loose about the khaki uniform with the black belt. The uniform of the army was so tight-fitting. Perhaps the whistle-chain and the truncheon improved this and the red-and-blue turban was nice, but—he lifted his hand to caress the folds of his head-dress and to adjust it, as it was heavy and got soaked with the sweat that flowed from his fuming scalp burdened by long hair on the lower edges. . . .

The sun poured down a flood of fire on the earth, and it seemed as if the desolate fields covered with dense brown thickets and stalks of grass and cacti were crackling like cinders and would soon be reduced to ashes. A partridge hummed in its nest somewhere and a dove cooed from the tree overhead, giving that depth to the shade which fills the air with long, endless silences and with the desolate peace of loneliness.

Mangal Singh drifted a few steps from where he was standing and halted on a spot where the shade was thicker than it was anywhere else under the kikar trees. And, blowing a hot breath, he cupped his palms over the knob of his stave and leaned his chin on the knuckles of his joined hands and stood contemplating the scene with half-closed eyes like a dog who rests his muzzle on his front paws and lies in wait for his prey.

Layers of white-sheeted mist floated past his eyes in the sun-soaked fields, the anguish of a thousand heat-signed bushes, while the parched leaves of the hanging boughs of the wayside trees rustled at the touch of a scorching breeze.

One breath, a thousand hopes, they say, and there never comes a day without evening—but it would be very difficult to walk down to the barracks through this terrible heat. And he wished his duty was not up, that someone could fetch his food for him and that he could borrow a charpai from the octroi and go to sleep in the grove of neem trees by the garden of Rais Jagjiwan Das, or sit and talk to the grass-cutter's wife who had breasts like turnips. Only Rahmat-Ullah had an eye on her too, and he was sure to be here, as he preferred the desolate afternoon, thinking that he might get a chance when no one was about.

'I will have to walk back to the lines,' he muttered to himself and yawned. He felt heavy and tired at the prospect and his legs seemed to weaken from the knowledge of the unending trudge of three miles. He shook his head and tried to be alert, but the invisible presence of some overwhelming force seemed to be descending on him and his heavy-lidded eyes were closing against his will. He took a deep breath and made another effort to open his eyes wide through the drowsy stupor of the shade that weighed down from the trees. For a moment his body steadied and his eyes half opened. But how hateful was the glare, and how cruel, how meaningless, was life outside. . . . And what peace, what quiet below the trees, beneath the eyes. . . .

If a God should be standing here he could not help closing his eyes for a minute, he felt; and sleep came creeping into his bones with a whiff of breeze that was like a soft beauty retreating coyly before the thousand glares of the torrid sun which burnt so passionately above the silent fields. . . . The heat seemed to be melting the fat in his head and to be blinding his eyes, and he let himself be seduced by the placid stillness into a trance of half-sleep. . . .

Through sleepy eyes he was conscious of the whispering elements as he dozed, and his body still stood more or less erect, though his head was bent on the knuckles of his hand above the stave, and the corners of his mouth dribbled slightly. . . .

'Shoop. . .shoop. . .shoop. . .' a snake seemed to lash his face at the same time as he saw the soothing vision of a dim city through the stealthy corners of whose lanes he was passing suavely into a house was effaced. . . .

'Shoop. . .shoop. . . .'

He came too suddenly and saw Thanedar Abdul Kerim standing before him, his young face red with anger under the affected Afghan turban, his tall lanky form tight-stretched, a cane in his hand, and his bicycle leaning against his legs. . . .

'Wake up! Wake up, you ox of a Sikh! Is it because it is past twelve that your senses have left you?

Mangal reeled, then steadied himself, his hands climbing automatically to his turban which had been shaken by the Inspector's onslaught.

'Shoop. . .shoop,' the cane struck his side again and stung his skin like a hundred scorpions. And a welter of abuse fell upon his ears: 'Bahin chod, the D.S.P. might have passed, and you are supposed to be on *duty*. Wake up and come to your senses, Madar chod!'

Quite involuntarily Mangal's right hand left the turban and shot up to his forehead in a salute, and his thick, trembling lips phewed some hot stale breath: 'Huzoor Mai-bap.'

'You eat the bread of illegality,' the Thanedar shouted. 'I will be reprimanded and my promotion stopped, you swine!'

And he lifted his cane to strike Mangal again, but the sepoy was shaking with fright so that his stave dropped from his hand.

Mangal bent and picked up his lathi.

'Go and be on your point-duty!' ordered the Thanedar sternly and, putting his foot on the pedal, rode shakily away on his bicycle.

Mangal walked out of the shade, his shins and thighs still trembling and his heart thumping in spite of himself, though he was less afraid than conscience-stricken for neglecting his duty.

The heat of the sun made the skin of his face smart with a sharp pain where the perspiration flowed profusely down his neck. He rubbed his hand across it and felt the sweat tingle like a raw wound.

He shook himself and his head twitched, and he looked about in order to see if anyone had seen him being beaten. He wanted to bear the pain like a man. But his eyes, startled by the suddenness with which they had opened, were full of a boiling liquid that melted into fumes as he raised his head.

His throat was parched dry and he coughed with an effort so that his big brown face above the shaggy beard reddened. Then he paused to spit on the road and felt his legs trembling and shaking more than ever. He twisted his face in the endeavour to control his limbs and lunged forward. . . .

'Ohe, may you die, ohe asses, ohe, may you die,' came a voice from behind him.

As he turned round he saw a herd of donkeys come stampeding up the road in a wild rush, which became wilder as their driver trotted fast behind them in an attempt to keep them from entering the Mall Road at that pace.

For a moment the cloud of dust the herd had raised on the sides of the deeply rutted Vadala Road obscured Mangal's view of the man, but then suddenly he could hear him shouting: 'Ohe, may you die, asses!'

Mangal ran with his stave upraised in a wild scurry towards the driver of the stampeding donkeys, scattering them helter-skelter till some of them cantered the more quickly into the Mall and the others turned back and come to a standstill. He caught the driver up before the man had escaped into a ditch by the banana field. And, grinding a half-expsessed curse between his teeth, he struck him with his stave hard, hard, harder, so that the blows fell edgewise on a donkey's neck, on the driver's arms, on a donkey's back, on a donkey's head, on the man's legs. . . .

'Oh, forgive, Sarkar, it is not my fault,' the man shouted in an angry, indignant voice while he rubbed his limbs and spread his hands to ward off more blows.

'You, son of a dog,' hissed Mangal as he struck again and again, harder and harder, as if he had gone mad, till his stave seemed to ring as a bamboo stick does when it is splitting into shreds.

(From *The Barbers' Trade Union and other Stories*, Jonathan Cape, London, 1944.)

2. BHABANI BHATTACHARYA

Bhabani Bhattacharya was born in Bhagalpur, Bihar, in 1906. He studied history at the University of Patna, and from there went to the University of London to graduate with a Ph. D. in 1934. While a student in England, he contributed articles to British periodicals, and on his return to India in 1935 he began writing for Indian papers and magazines. From 1949-50 he worked as Press Attache to the Indian Embassy in Washington, and from 1950-52 as Assistant Editor of *The Illustrated Weekly of India* (Bombay). Among positions he has held are Secretary, Tagore Commemorative Society (New Delhi, 1959-60); Consultant, Ministry of Education (New Delhi, 1961-67), and Senior Specialist, East-West Center (Honolulu, 1969-70). He has also been a Visiting Professor at the University of Hawaii (Honolulu) and has lectured widely in the United States, Europe, Australia and New Zealand. He lives in St. Louis County (Missouri, USA) and devotes his time to writing.

Bhabani Bhattacharya published his first novel *So Many Hungers!* in 1947—a harrowing tale about the 1943 Bengal famine. He followed it up with *Music for Mohini* (1952), *He Who Rides a Tiger* (1954), *A Goddess Named Gold* (1960), *Shadow from Ladakh* (1966) for which he received the Sahitya Akademi Award, *Steel Hawk and Other Stories* (1968), and his most recent *A Dream in Hawaii* (1978). He believes that art and criticism of life go together, and his best works reveal a happy blending of the two. His novels have been translated into fifteen European and several Asian languages.

He Who Rides a Tiger—Described by *The Times* (London) as 'a rare and beautiful novel,' *He Who Rides a Tiger* is a hard-hitting social satire on the one hand, and a story of unfaltering love and compassion on the other. A terrible famine is raging through Bengal, and Kalo, a blacksmith, is forced to flee his village to make a living and support Chandra Lekha—his only daughter whom he adores above all things in life. An ill-fated moment during his journey to Calcutta sees him in jail, and when he is released he finds there is no decent way of making a living. After a spell at clearing the city streets of human corpses, victims of the famine, he becomes a procurer for whore-houses so that he can send his daughter her means of support. Ironically, in one of those houses he finds the terrified Lekha. A vice vendor, feigning to be an emissary from her father, had enticed her to the city.

Recovering from the shock, the embittered Kalo resolves to take his revenge on society. He assumes the Brahminic name of Mangal Adhikari to hide his low-caste origin and dupes people into building a Shiva temple with himself as its revered chief priest. He and his daughter start a new life and for the time being there is no turning back. Viswanath, a starving blacksmith, is hired to work in the temple grounds; Bikash Mukherjee, Kalo's cellmate who calls himself Biten (B 10), joins the temple community. Both these anti-establishment men are for Kalo a reminder of his submerged, half-forgotten social concerns. Meanwhile, Motilal, a rich merchant of easy morals who has been backing the temple with his money, sets his eyes on the beautiful Chandra Lekha. He wants to get rid of his fourth wife, Radha, and marry Chandra Lekha. And he also wants to vest her with an aura of divinity. So Chandra Lekha, an unwilling collaborator with her father, finds herself becoming the 'Mother of Sevenfold Bliss.' He who rides a tiger cannot dismount—so goes an ancient proverb. But Kalo, conscious of Chandra Lekha's resistance as also of his own inner revulsion, summons up enough moral strength to dismount the tiger of the lie he has been riding. At a ceremony to install Chandra Lekha to her elevated position, he tells the assemblage about the deception he has practised, and with his daughter walks away to an uncertain future.

What follows is the climactic last chapter of the novel:

He Who Rides A Tiger

The *yagna* was to begin at the sacred hour of dawn. All preparations had been completed the day before. A hundred large cans of *ghee* had arrived in a wagon and lay stored, with stacks of kindling. The high moment of the *yagna* was the great sacrificial fire, fed only with the purest *ghee*, rare in these lean days. As the fumes rose in a scented cloud, the *pujari*, conducting the ceremony, chanted the *mantra* assisted by eight priests who formed a circle and blended their voices with his. The chant made a sombre cry:

'Thou who art the secret breath in all created beings,
Hail to thee, Mother, and hail, and hail, hail!'
Again:
'Thou who art the joyous light in all created beings,
Hail to thee, Mother, and hail, and hail, hail!'
And again:
'Thou who art the core of bliss in all created beings,
Hail to thee, Mother, and hail, and hail, hail!'

The Mother would wear yellow silk, her arms adorned with conch shell bangles mounted in gold, around her throat a seven-stringed *har* of unblemished pearls. She would be seated on a strip of carpet beside the sacrificial fire, the heat of the flames giving her face warmth and color like the flush of the dawn goddess. The scented fumes would be part of her indrawn breath, passing deep into her body and mingling with her blood. The ceremony would continue all day, without a break, until sunset.

Formal invitations had been handed to the city's temples and to pundits renowned for their knowledge of ancient lore. All true Brahmins were welcome to see the installation of the Mother. This was to be a day of days in the great city's spiritual life. Motichand, wearing his false modesty well, seemed open-handed with his cash and his time.

A weather-gray canvas awning in the temple yard kept out the sun. The ground, up to the foot of the Lotus Pavilion, was covered with thick cotton *satrenji* woven on handlooms in the city's central jail. The Pavilion itself was reserved for guests of rank, a rich blue Kashmir carpet clothing its marble floor. Satin cushions were strewn around to support arms, fat round pillows to support backs. No Western style chairs were allowed on this occasion which had to follow tradition exactly—except in one respect. Motichand believed in speeches, English-fashion. They had benefited him in his public life, won him a seat in the Legislative Council, in fact. But he would not be the first speaker. That honor would fall to Mangal Adhikari. Motichand would be last. With his wit, his knowledge of what his audience would like to hear, he would be the commanding figure of the day, for Motichand was the hundred-branched tree and Mangal was his shadow. He was the moving force; Mangal, his instrument. Mangal, too, had his value. The day was not far off when this man, uncouth but shrewd in some ways, was to be Motichand's father-in-law.

Often, these days, Motichand had felt abashed at the game he was playing. Not once had he countered the wish of his fellow trustees to install Mangal's daughter as Mother of Sevenfold Bliss. He had, in truth, worked honestly to make the ceremony effective. The trustees had a surprise in store! They would not like it. But Motichand was big enough to play the game by his own rules.

He had set his heart on the girl. He would marry her. She was willing, so he had heard. He had his ears everywhere. The pigheaded Mangal who had at first taken a foolish attitude—he, clearly, was bent on making good use of the Mother—would have to accept the inevitable. Odd to think that he, Mangal, and the trustees were, at heart, one! For the meaningful fact was that Motichand was not going to marry the Mother of Sevenfold Bliss. She would have to relinquish her spiritual role in good time to become a mere mortal's fifth wife!

She had decided well. At her age it was far more fun to be simply woman! If only she realized that she would be the spouse of a man with strict moral standards unheard of in these days of evil.

His future relations with Radha were still unsettled. His mind was still open for a solution to that tricky point which should be decided by a new wife herself! Was it not up to her to hold her man with a woman's artful devices?

Radha had played too readily into his hands. She had given no trouble. That was his luck, for he could not treat Radha as he had his former wives. He had never suspected that she cared so much for her vermilion mark of wifehood. She knew the true value of her husband! Full credit had to be given, however, to the yellow-clad thug at the Kali temple. Motichand with his deep-seeing eye had spotted the right man. Radha was no fool, but she had trusted the thug. All glory to the holy ash! Of course the thug had overpriced his services. A thousand rupees! Not that Motichand regretted the expense. He had only to give one look at Chandra Lekha and feel the gush of pleasure in his veins to be assured that the expense had been worthwhile. He could never have fought it out alone with Radha and won.

The city would lose its Mother of Sevenfold Bliss, but his own prestige would touch the sky. Perhaps he and his spouse could make a partnership of her divine role and continue it together?

A staggering idea. Only his inventive mind could have conceived it. He saw himself in the new role, unique in spiritual annals. For a moment he was so taken with his own noble image he could almost have touched the dust on his feet in reverence. Then he burst out laughing, his teeth shining. It was a grand idea, but not practical. Even if he wore the saintly cloak, which would be far from easy, there would be hurdles. His business, for one. He was going to retire from business, and it would be unwise to run it through the hands of a manager or partner. In any case, it would take the zest from his life.

That reminded him of another problem—his present manager and father-in-law. With Radha gone, her father would nurse a secret anger and cease to be worthy of trust. He must be replaced. By whom? The assistant manager, Chotalal? That point, too, had to be settled. Thakurdas must be given a sudden notice of discharge, lest he should plan mischief. . . . So many tiresome things had to be fixed up.

The hour was at hand.

The guests of rank had risen early and hastened to the temple in their cars. Even Sir Abalabandhu, a late riser, had turned up in time. A hundred priests and pundits stood by, watching the feeding of the sacrificial fire, Everything was in order. Everything was set for Mangal Adhikari's speech.

As Chandra Lekha, with her father climbed the steps of the Pavilion, Motichand handed her the seven-stringed necklace of unblemished pearls which his last two wives had worn. Lekha's face was serene but her eyes, hard. Motichand understood.

'Be easy,' he wanted to tell her. 'Not for long will you wear saffron. Your woman's heart feels choked and rebels. Don't I know your feelings, I who have built a home with four wives, one by one? Have patience, wife-to-be, till the sun rises on the golden day of our betrothal.'

Mangal, he noticed, was brooding. His eyes were deep in their sockets, as if he had not slept for many nights. He did not even greet the visitors of rank. He seemed remote.

'What's wrong with Mangal?' Sir Abalabandhu whispered to his friend. 'He looks like a ghost!'

Motichand whispered back, 'He is overwhelmed. He has traveled a long way. It is enough to soften a fellow's head.'

The white-clad *pujari*, wearing old fashioned wooden sandals, walked to the Pavilion, his head up.

'The sacrificial fire burns high.'

Motichand walked to the edge of the Pavilion and faced the assemblage, his palms humbly joined at his chest.

'Friends and brothers, pray be seated.'

There was a hum of approval as the crowd sat down, legs crossed. The distinguished men in the Pavilion pulled up fat satin cushions to ease their backs and bellies.

'It is my proud privilege to ask the maker of this temple, who saw the god in his dream, to give us a few be-jeweled words, bearing a true message. Friends and brothers, do you approve?'

'We do! We do!'

Kalo sat on, hunched over, yet a while. Slowly he rose to his feet. His glance lay on the assemblage and his hand fumbled over the shiny dome of his head. He seemed to sway a little.

After another long moment of silence, he began.

'I am no fit person to speak to you.' The words came haltingly. He paused. 'Of knowledge I have little. *Mantra* and *tantra* are not within my understanding. The holy words. . . .'

'We hear you, Adhikari, we hear you.' A voice from the audience encouraged him in a friendly way.

Then Kalo seemed to waken from his half-sleep. A sudden force took hold of him. The morning sun spilled through the marble grille of the Pavilion and slanted behind him, deepening the shadows on his face.

'The holy words have been taboo to folks of my caste for thousands and thousands of years, ever since they were invented, ever since our way of life started. And I, who stand before you, I who made Shiva's abode.' His tone was low but aggressive. 'I who made this temple was not born a Brahmin.'

Shouts of laughter greeted the statement. The assemblage rocked with fun. People turned to each other, grinning. 'Have you ever heard a better joke?' 'That's no joke. It's the humility of a fulfilled spirit at peace with the world, don't you understand?' 'There is a deep meaning behind the meaning.'

His eyes fixed and smoldering, Kalo surveyed his audience. His hour had struck, the hour toward which he had been inexorably plodding through the travail of the past weeks, of the past months.

When Lekha declared her will to marry a man she could never love or respect, Kalo knew she was repaying him. Did she think he would buy even life itself on those terms! Had he gone down so much in her eyes?

He understood what had driven them so far apart. He saw himself and trembled.

He was riding a tiger and could not dismount. He had sat astraddle, half-resigned but helpless while the beast prowled or reced at will. Yet even as he rode, he had been aware all the time that there was no way but to kill the tiger.

The idea of giving up ease, comfort, security for the hard living in Jharna town had frightened him. It had made him feel feeble and his legs had pressed against the flanks of his mount, tightening his seat.

But the need to kill the tiger grew because of a strength in him, a strength he had never known before. It was the strength which comes of seeing people as they are. He had looked deep into the faces of his superiors, inhabitants of a 'higher' world whose very shadow had once struck him into abject humility. But he had become their equal and he had sized them up.

Everything that had happened to the simple *kamar* of Jharna town had slowly worked into the texture of his being. The jailhouse, the harlot-house, the temple. Anguish and shame and exultation. Never again would the smith be despised, mocked, trampled upon. Never again. For the fetters of his mind had been cut. The look in his eyes was clear and undazzled.

The next phase came when Biten stirred him to the depths, not by words, simply by example. An example of smothering one's own heart in loyalty to an idea.

The crisis of mind Biten had predicted for him would perhaps have come upon Kalo anyhow, but Chandra Lekha, bent on destroying herself, forced his decision. His hand had at last attained the power of his will. It would plunge a dagger into the tiger's heart.

And here, with the *yagna* fire lit, the air thick with frankincense and holy chantings, was the appropriate moment for the kill. Even Lekha did not know. Kalo was not without a dramatic sense. And there was no more dramatic or irrevocable way to redeem himself.

'You laugh? Well you may. Laugh till the hard truth sinks to your stomachs and rolls there like an iron ball. Laugh, brothers and friends.'

He had to pause to ease his shortness of breath.

'I am no fit person to speak to you, as I have said. That is just a way of talk. Of knowledge I have little, as I have said. That is a way of talk again. In my blood and bones I have learned a lesson. A lesson bigger than your *tantra* and *mantra*. Now listen well, priests and pundits, listen to the truth.' The voice throbbed. 'I have installed a false god, for there was no dream at all. I have made you commit sacrilege and blacken your faces. There is no expiation for you—maybe the writers of the holy books have not prescribed any, for they could not have dreamed that such a thing could happen! Some of you have been wild-eyed with wrath because I gave shelter to a homeless little boy of unknown caste. A down-trodden *kamar* has been in charge of your inmost souls, souls corrupt with caste and cash!'

Bewildered, too dazed to speak or act, the crowd was wrapped in awful silence. A lone cry wailed through the spell, 'What disaster is this? No, no, it cannot be true.'

'No?' There was a glow of anger in Kalo's metallic face. He clutched the yellow scarf on his body, pulled it off and bared his chest. He wore no sacred thread.

Five hundred pairs of eyes stared at the broad bare chest in fascinated horror. They could not look away.

In the tense silence a low murmur began, like a deep hiss. The crowd was like a serpent being prodded awake after its long winter sleep.

'So you know at last. I am a *kamar* from afar. Hunger drove me from my native earth. Hunger took me to jail. From there I walked into hell itself. I saw the face of Evil. I asked myself a question, I who had been content with my lot, my humble place in life. I puzzled over all that had happened to me until the answer came: Nothing is as true as falseness! The more false you are, to yourself and to others, the more true you become! The rest of the answer is' Evil is to be faced and fought with its own knives!'

He paused and turned a sharp glance on the people on the platform. Sir Abalabandhu had a peculiar smile, as if he were enjoying the situation. Motichand had a dazed look. Jogesh was wiping his eye-glasses and his hands shook. And Chandra Lekha—Kalo let his eyes rest upon her.

Her expression was one of rapt worship. He had seen it in her face when, as a child, she had watched him work, shaping a horse-shoe with fire and iron. He had seen it when she woke once in the middle of the night and caught him poring over her geography book. But he had not seen it for a long time and it ran through him like steel or like honey and gave him even greater strength to destroy in fury and create in love. He could shake the earth with his hands or endure agony in silence. He felt unbearably happy.

Again he faced the crowd which was still in the grip of shock.

'So it was that, first of all, I made myself a Brahmin. The sacred thread lay across my chest. Do not dare judge me or call me a swindler. I have been as Brahminic as any of you! Then I performed a trick of magic.' He paused a few moments and new zest enlivened his voice. 'Many tricks of magic are performed everyday by my good friends here, but this one was my own. I chiseled a piece of stone in Shiva's shape. I buried it at this spot where the temple now stands, and under the stone was gram, two *seers* of gram. As I watered the earth, the gram underneath swelled and pushed the stone up to the surface. People stood by, watching the miracle happen.'

The serpent, now fully awake, was swaying its hood and its fangs were charged with venom.

'The temple began. The temple grew. Big men came forward with their bags of money.' Kalo spoke on in the voice of a snake-charmer. 'They had their own motives, their own little tricks of magic. They were not content, though, with mine, for they, too, were magicians and presently they performed tricks as baffling as mine.'

Kalo held his breath for the final thrust of his dagger and the assemblage as one man caught its breath. Kalo looked again at the rapt worship on Chandra Lekha's face.

'Out of a simple-hearted teen-age girl who made no claims to holiness, a girl like ten million others in Bengal, they created a lie as big as the lie inside the temple. They created the Mother of Sevenfold Bliss.'

The *pujari*, seated in the front row of the audience, sprang to his feet, as if released by a coiled spring, and yelled like a madman 'The evil one has made us eat filth. The evil one has doomed us for all our lives to come.' His long gray beard jerked. 'Let him pay!'

The audience gave full-throated shouts. 'The rougue! The *shaitan*! Beat him up. Break every bone in his carcass.

'He has made us eat filth...the *shaitan* out of hell-pit.... He has doomed us to suffering for life after life..., The evil thing in human shape....' Voices hoarse with rage crossed and blended. Fists gestured in the air.

Kalo was speaking again.

'Wait! he shouted at the top of his voice. 'For the story is not ended.'

But the spell was broken. The people were shouting mad threats though uncertain how to act. Motichand beckoned to the *pujari* who went to the platform's edge. 'Yes, yes' he nodded when Motichand had spoken in a heated whisper.

'I shall tell you about a second and greater truth I discovered, because of which I stand before you today,' Kalo began again.

A stone struck his bare chest. He stopped speaking. The exalted crowd on the platform ran for cover behind the marble colonnades.

Blood dripped down Kalo's chest but he made no effort to wipe it off. Chandra Lekha threw her arms around him, shielding him with her body. Kalo pushed her to the side where he made her stay. He stood motionless on the platform as though he were carved of solid rock.

'That woman, the shameless creature.... her looks bespeak a harlot. In fact, we have often doubted her origin.... My wife could see through her and she said to me the other day....

'That waif is her bastard son, be sure.'

'*Kamar*? His skin, his features, bespeak the meanest Untouchable, a *chamar*, cobbler, or a sweeper.'

'May all three be burned by lightning from the sky!'

'May their rotten carcasses be food for vultures.'

Kalo, gazing down at the excited faces, did not even feel angry. He felt stronger than all of them together. His passion had subsided and a great calm was in him. His face was sad and his eyes softened strangely with pity.

The *pujari* was shouting, 'Brothers, pray don't throw brickbats. We have guests on the Pavilion. There are other ways....'

'We'll tear them limb from limb.... The *shaitan* and the harlot-woman....They've doomed us for all our lives to come. Hang them from the banyan tree!'

As tension mounted, an undertone of protest was growing slowly in the far back rows among the uninvited guests who sat on the grass or stood crowded together. They were common people—street sweepers, rickshaw runners, coolies from the neighboring Heema Soap factory—who had come to see the *tamasha*, the spectacle. They had been bewildered by the proceedings and for a time could make nothing of the situation. But Kalo's words had sunk into their minds and touched something. Those who were quick to grasp explained the facts to their slow-witted friends. Eyebrows shot up. Murmurs grew excited.

'What a wonder! He has made the mighty ones eat dirt!'

'The mighty ones with noses in the sky. They tread upon us as if we were earthworms, less than earthworms, for those worms don't cast pollution as some of us do by our presence or touch.

'As if God were Brahmin by caste!'

'As if *chamars* must not earn merit lest they go to heaven and jostle shoulders with the caste folks!'

So the talk went in the back rows, and the men in the Pavilion regained their poise.

'The rascal must be brought to law.' An eminent judge peered from behind one colonnade to confer with a famous lawyer who was hiding behind another.

'A clear case of fraud.' The lawyer's mind was running over sections of the Criminal Code.

'If that charge fails, the Government will have to step in and use preventive detention,' said a superior official of the Secretariat. 'We can't let the people's morale be tampered with in wartime.'

'The people's anger may yet express itself in direct action,' said the gray-haired politician with a sidelong look at the crowd. 'And we can't help it if it disposes of those two enemies of society.'

Behind a marble column at the farthest corner of the Pavilion Sir Abalabandhu's face looked tortured as he tried to control his laughter.

'Marvelous!' he burst out at last. What business sense! What method! Why aren't there one or two men like the blacksmith in my office?' He gave Motichand, who stood at his side, a clap on the shoulder. 'Brother, after all, he is your discovery!'

Group after group in the crowd urged violent action but the men in the back rows continued their talk.

'He has taught them a lesson they will hold in their bellies.'

'He has given them three good kicks on the buttocks for the filth they have always thrown on us.'

'He who has been master of the temple is our kin, our own brother.'

Out of the crowd, now swaying with passionate anger, two men pushed forward, elbowing their way to the Pavilion steps where they turned round as though standing guard.

Kalo wanted to yell at the top of his voice. His eyes lit up. Biten! Viswanath! They had come back. They had come back in time to hear him, to see him drive his steel deep into the tiger. The scum of the earth had hit back, hit back where it hurt.

Chandra Lekha's face was rapturous and yet aflush with remembrance.

Had he forgiven her for her madness of a moment? If only he had an inkling what he had made her suffer by going away. If he knew that *he* had given her to the temple and to the Mother of Sevenfold Bliss.

At this time the unthinkable happened. From the back rows of the common folks came a shout. 'Victory to our brother!'

It was a lone, strained voice but it concretized feeling. It shouted what hundreds of others now had the courage to shout. 'Victory to our brother!' It came like an explosion.

The Brahmins under the canvas awning swung round as if at a command. Those on the Pavilion were astounded. How had it happened? How had the impostor turned the tide in his favor! Had he posted his own men in the crowd against trouble? Where were the police?

'Victory to our brother!' With each repetition the mass of shouting voices gathered power, gathered fire in a crescendo of wrath. 'Victory to our brother!'

Kalo was as stunned as the Brahmins. What were these people who were cheering *him*? One look at the shouting men and he knew.

'Motichand!' Sir Abalabandhu called, his face dead serious. The two conferred.

'Victory to our brother!' It was now a war cry.

Kalo knew that his battle was won at last.

Biten, you hear?

Viswanath, you hear?

How could one deceive one's blood and bone—ever?

And Chandra Lekha felt the exultation within her too overwhelming to bear.

Baba, the people cry-victory to you!

Baba, a hundred temples are worth less to us than this moment!

Baba, after this, whatever happens to us, wherever we go, we can never again be unhappy or defeated.

Panic finally seized the Brahmins. They were on their feet, ready to run. Hooligans stood around, daggers hidden in their waistcloths, *Fly, fly.* . . .

Motichand hastened to the front of the Pavilion. He joined his hands at his chest, praying to be heard.

His voice was heavy, subdued. Peace and order had to be maintained at any price, he said. Violence was out of place everywhere, and nowhere so much as on holy premises, even when there was extreme provocation. The godless *kumar* who had made a mockery of the supreme deity would surely get his punishment but it would have to come from the divine hand. That hand was already at work. Had it not forced the blacksmith to vomit his foul confession? It was not easy to forgive him but the spiritual leaders of the great city, the pride of India and of the world, could not let themselves be carried away by bitter passion. . . .

'Come, Chandra Lekha.'

Out of the nine-petaled stone lotus Kalo walked down to the soft earth, holding his daughter's hand. He stopped, as if questioning Biten with a glance, Biten's response came in a low, impassioned murmur.

'You have chosen, my friend, You have triumphed over those others—and over yourself. What you have done just now will steel the spirit of hundreds and thousands of us. Your story will be a legend of freedom, a legend to inspire and awaken.'

Knit by a common feeling, they held each other with their eyes until Kalo smiled faintly and shook his head.

'No, Bikash Mukherji, the conquest is yours.'

He turned and resumed walking. He cut a path between right grim faces with his large fist held in front of him.

'The pearls!' Motichand, in mid-speech, gave a frantic scream.

Chandra Lekha had forgotten the pearls. She jerked the necklace off her throat, flung it on Motichand's outstretched arm, and walked on.

Biten and Viswanath followed a few paces behind, stopping at the far edge of the crowd.

'They will need each other and none else at this moment,' said Biten.

Viswanath nodded.

Kalo, alone with his daughter, passed out of the gateway of the temple.

(From *He who rides the tiger*, New York, Crown Publishers, 1954, pp. 223-45)

Steel Hawk

THE news came at sunrise, charging the air with echoes, like the beat of a drum. Men sped off from the fields, wiping earth-stained hands on their loin-cloths. Women shouted for their children as they hurried past, their voices swift and shrill. And the children danced with joy, clapping each other on the back, yelling:

'It's the flying wonder, you hear? We'll go ariding in the sky!

'We'll touch the clouds, you hear? We'll squeeze clouds in our fists to make rain!

For in the large meadow on the western edge of the Indian village stood the flying wonder, the sun beating on its wings, the crowd around swelling every minute.

Bishan, the carter, had yoked his pair of bullocks and was coming along in hot haste. He cajoled the animals, prodded them with a short, thick rod, and once or twice pulled each one by the tail. 'Tchuk, tchuk! Run! Do not fall asleep, dear brother!'

There was not an eye flick of time to lose. The flying wonder would be gone any moment. Who would expect such a chance to cross a man's life twice? Those wond rs were seen on the sky-ways often enough—strange passing birds in the far blue; at night time they were pilgrim stars! But then here was one squatting afield, a mere wagon tied to earth! Why was it here? Just to rest for a bit on solid earth? Or could there be some mystery behind it, some hidden purpose?

The wheels of wood thwacked the deep dust of the road. The bullocks raced, their heavy flanks quaking, their heads dizzy with speed. 'Tchuk, tchuk! Run hard, gentlemen, run till you lose your breath!'

As the cart was passing the Balcony of Knowledge, where the village school-teacher lived, Kamini, the teacher's young wife, hailed from the doorway: 'Oxcart, will you take us to the meadow on which the wonder of wonders has descended?

Red dust clung to her bare feet. One hand held a half-drawn veil, the other clutched the arm of Babla, her six-year old daughter.

'What fare, Ox-cart?' she added, as the vehicle pulled up alongside.

'Why, Mother, I'm going there to fill my own eyes. How can I charge you a fare?'

The cartman's eyes turned, rose to the thatched kitchen roof, his face beaming, 'A-ha, what a pumpkin vine you've raised, what tendrils, lithe and strong, what yellow bells of blooms!'

'The first-fruits of that plant will be yours.'

The bargain settled, Kamini climbed in at the cart's rear, with her daughter.

The cow-bells jingled and the cart trekked down the pathway to the meadow, skirting a shadowed mango grove, and turned into a lane between fields of paddy, a red tape zigzagging through sweeps of vivid yellow. The tall paddy, with full-kernelled grain, drooped under the weight of the wind.

'Never will *she* set her two eyes on this wonder!' the cartman spoke softly, as if to himself, shaking his close-cropped head with sadness. 'What evil fate that gout holds her bones on this day, of all days! The whole village sees the wonder; she alone is denied.'

'Who, Ox-cart?'

'Old Grandma, poor soul. Mad about tricky machines, stark mad! Same today as in her long-ago days, when the rail road first came this way.'

'Railroad?' said Kamini, in surprise. 'The railroad came this way countless years ago.'

The cartman smiled. 'Grandma is countless years old, isn't she? It happened when she was 14 or 15....'

'What happened?' cried Kamini. 'Tell me, cartman!' her voice pleaded.

'A railway station was built at Choorni, one hour's walk from our Sonamitti.'

'Yes. What then?'

'Grandma was 14 or 15. Wed a short time.'

'I am listening,' said Kamini, for the cartman had paused again.

'Grandma had seen fire-engines roll past, sooty smoke belching out of the squat nostril. Now at last she could see one standing by, big and quiet as an elephant. She could reach out with her hand, feel the iron skin. Grandpapa read her mind and took her to Choorni one day in his cart.'

And now Bishan warmed to his story. He neglected his oxen, turned his face towards his listener and let his voice go faster: 'Grandpapa took her to Choorni station one day. They heard the rumble like twenty thunders and the fire-engine came hotfoot, a monster, with coach after coach of metal and wood, all ashine with paint and glass. For full five breaths Grandma was dead still. The train wouldn't wait long, so Grandpapa warned her, and she at once came back to life. She, first of all, bent low to look at the hundred wheels. Then she walked to the engine, its barrel body all oily with the sweat of toil and moil too one good look at it and also at the man in blue tunic and trouser who drove the monster. She turned back, peering in here, there, everywhere, to see the lights that needed no oil to

Steel Hawk

make them burn, the fans that needed no hand to stir a breeze, and she turned her eyes this way and that, at this and that passenger, woman, child, man.....

'At last, when the fire-engine gave a long "coo-oo" and started to move off, "whoosh-whoosh-whoosh," coach after coach going fast and smooth, as if gliding on glass, Grandma was dead still again.

'It was a good bit of time before she found her tongue. She turned round to Grandpapa and said:

'Truly, such a thing exists! To see this I must have earned merit by a hundred and one good deeds!'

'And she closed her eyes and joined her palms to her forehead, saluting the image of majesty. Grandpapa burst out laughing but his eyes must have been wet. Two or three days later, they went again to Choorni Station, and this time they bought tickets and rode on the train. They rode to the next stop. They walked back home.'

Bishan paused a moment, returning from his mind-picture of the past, and his voice came huskily: 'Old she is, and as crazy still as in her long-ago days.'

'The sadness that she will not see the flying wonder!' Kamini shook her head with pity. 'Athrill she would have been, as before.'

'She bade me rush and see this machine. She will see it afterwards with *my* eyes. She will want to know everything—how it looks, how it smells. . . .'

There was a silence. The cartman prodded his bullocks. 'Hey, brothers of an ass, run! Run hard till you lose our breath! Faster, gentlemen, faster!'

The crowd came into view. The cart drew up in a minute. Bishan unyoked the animals.

'Make way for the mother from the Balcony of Knowledge!' he said, pushing his way gently through the assembled people watching with bated breath.

So small! Bishan felt quite disappointed. A mere grasshopper! So different from what one saw on the skypath! A comic figure with two wheels—as though paved streets ran up there in the sky' A hawk with no legs but wheels! And the wings looked much too stiff to fold or even to flap! A tail with fishlike fin! Blades on the snout, good weapons to fight with! In a battle of the air, the pilot could wield the blades to gore the foe in the guts!

Grandma had not missed much, anyhow, Bishan felt relieved and happy. But, then, he must'nt take away her fond belief. 'Grandma,' he would say, 'the air wagon is twice as big as the fire-engine. Its white body bristles all over with guns, porcupine-like. It is a true fighter, Grandma! It has the soldier's smell, and even to look at it is to feel fear.'

Grandma, listening intently, would wag her head with satisfaction. 'Just what I thought. The Ramayana, our epic of the olden times, pictures the flying chariot that existed then. Bishan, boy, life is a Great Wheel! It spins slowly in the Stream of Time, a finger's width in a hundred years! Things on top get lost to the view with the Wheel's turning, but, as time flows on, they rise again!'

'Grandma must not lose the flying wonder of her fancy,' Bishan said to himself, decisively.

The machine was about to take off. And no one yet had an inkling why it had landed here.

Men and women and children held their breath as the pilot smilingly waved his hand at them, turned round and stepped up to his seat. Suddenly, the blades on the snout swung into motion with a zoom that grew more and more—at first a splutter of many sounds, then one big beat. As the machine darted and hopped into the air, the crowd first gasped, then broke into a clamour. Loud yells of cheering followed the machine as it climbed skywards.

'Ma', cried Babla, straining her eyes against the sun, 'what if birds attack the flying wonder? Fifty, twenty birds?"

'Birds have no malice, darling. They have clean thoughts, all except the crows, and crows cannot get so high.'

'What if a pack of ruffian crows gets so high, Ma?'

'Then the flying wonder will pour out fumes. The crows will drop down, a heap of feather and beak.'

The cartman was bemused as he was walking away, slow-footed. No, that Steel Hawk had not fallen short of Grandma's fancy. What had seemed on land a mere grosshopper grew into splendour up there in the sky. All the same.....

The bullocks were munching grass. The cartman yoked them back and stood, leaning over the hump of one animal. The Steel Hawk had great speed and went far faster than all winged creatures. All the same, why must speed greedily eat up the farness? Why ask to reach your journey's end in two hours or three?

Pondering, he could not make it out. Was it not more easeful to rattle along on the road? You could speak to the folks (and no folks to speak to on the skypath), stop and pluck a bloom from the fields or a sprig of tasty green gram, and you could do a hundred other things.

Why must speed greedily eat up the farness?

Grandma would know the answer; she was mad about tricky machines, stark mad. Grandma could look at the flying wonder and go ariding it in her fancy, zooming away mightily and shooting from sky to sky like a crazy star. Grandma had that sort of mind. She had it when she was young, and she still had it when her hair was without one black strand, all teeth gone, and sadness and pain written on her brow in each of a hundred wrinkles, graven deep.

Bishan twisted his face, feeling a tenderness in him and yet a superiority, a knowingness. Grandma's spirit was catching up with him! She who was of Yesterday was possessed by Today. Then how could one who was of Today be otherwise? Could one belong in one's mind to whatever time one liked? Could one, person ever exchange roots with another, exchange the breath in his nostrils?

He lifted his face skywards, his eyes hard with a kind of challenge.

What if *she* could be there, the aged Grandma, riding the Steel Hawk? And Bishan felt his heart swell. Wouldn't she be even more thrilled than when she saw the fire-engine for the first time; or when, two or three days later, she rode in one of the rumbling, rocking coaches?

Truly, such a thing exists! To see this I must have earned merit by a hundred and one good deeds!

And Bishan, shading his eyes with his palm and turning them to the far sky, surrendered himself to his fancy.... There she was, the aged Grandma, with her modern dream, riding the Steel Hawk, soaring atop!

'Ho, pilot brother, take heed lest you lose your bearings! Take heed lest you brush against a shooting star or move too close to the sun-god! Take heed lest you be pulled into the dark realm of baleful Saturn! Take heed lest you be doomed to wander forlorn on the skyways, never to return to earth! Take all heed, ho, pilot brother!'

Impatient cow-bells tinkled into his reverie while he leaned against the fat, white flanks of an ox, but his neck remained craned, his mind remote. For the cartman of Sonamitti village had yielded to the impulse of the age and was riding the Steel Hawk with his Grandma, zooming away mightily.

(From *The Steel Hawk and Other Stories*, Orient Paperbacks, New Delhi.)

3. RUTH PRAWER JHABVALA

Ruth Prawer Jhabvala was born in 1927 in Cologne, now in West Germany. Her Polish parentage, German upbringing and British schooling provide a cosmopolitan setting for her role as an author. She received her M.A. in English Literature from the University of London in 1951. She married an Indian architect, Cyrus H.S. Jhabvala, came to India in 1951 and settled down in Delhi. Her first novel, *To Whom She Will* was published in 1955, her second, *The Nature of Passion*, in 1956, and her third, *Esmond in India*, in 1958. *The Householder*, which was later made into a movie, appeared in 1960 and *A Backward Place*, an absorbing and socially stimulating work of fiction, in 1965. Jhabvala has also written excellent short stories, four collections of which have so far been published. But it was her novel, *Heat and Dust*, which won the prestigious Booker Memorial Prize in 1976 and made her internationally known. The same year also saw the publication of her latest collection of stories, *How I Became a Holy Mother*.

Jhabvala has a discerning eye for the changing pattern of urban life in modern India, especially in and around Delhi. She shows a considerable narrative power in drawing an ironic, comic, yet sympathetic, portrait of the middle classes. Her stories have appeared in *Encounter*, *The New Yorker* and other prestigious journals. Her major fiction, rated high by some, has also been criticised by others. She is undoubtedly a very skilful writer of domestic comedy with a penchant for irony and social satire. Her portrayal of India and Indian scene, though marked by detachment, has become somewhat controversial. Nevertheless, she is widely regarded as a major creative writer and a fine portrayer of the Indian scene.

A Backward Place brings out many subtle nuances of Jhabvala's art and life, especially her emotional and intellectual responses as a person and as a creative writer. In an essay, 'Living in India,' she writes: 'The most salient fact about India is that it is very poor and backward. There are so many things to be said about it but this must remain the basis of all of them.' Jhabvala is almost overwhelmed by this stark reality of India, which shows itself in her writing and in her view of life.

The controlling metaphor of *A Backward Place* encompasses the viewpoints of the various characters in the novel. India, especially the areas around Delhi, seems to the Europeans a kind of 'backward place'—a view unmistakably expressed in the utterances of Etta, the Hungarian beauty. The Hochstadts seem to go into raptures over India, although they are quite conscious of the differences between East and West.

In *A Backward Place*, Jhabvala explores one basic human relationship, that of Bal and Judy. Our awareness of it is either modified or expanded by other characters such as Sudhir, Jayakar, Mrs Kaul, Etta, Shanti, and Bhuaji. Judy, who has met Bal in London, is taken in by his handsome face and gaiety. Her cheerless domestic life in England is partly the cause of her being attracted to Bal and his blowsy spirits. Bal is a gay youth, who dreams of becoming a film star. He hangs around his film hero, Kishan Kumar, and neglects Judy and their son, Prithvi. Judy is passionately devoted to him, although she is aware of his failings. It is Judy's love that sustains their marital happiness, as also her being able to adapt herself to the trying conditions of the Hindu joint family situation. She identifies herself admirably with the lives of Bal and Shanti, her sister-in-law, and Bhuaji, an old pious woman. Judy, perhaps, is one of the few women characters in Jhabvala's fiction who strike a note of hope and affirmation in the face of the unexpected and sudden challenges of life.

Sudhir presents a study in contrast to Bal. A cultured Bengali youth, Sudhir is in-charge of the 'Cultural Dais.' Judy is his assistant and Mrs Kaul, a pompous society lady, is his Honorary Secretary. Sudhir is practical-minded although he appears to be rather pessimistic, while Bal is given to dreaming and fanciful illusions.

While 'the Cultural Dais' symbolises the culture of the sophisticated, or what may be called the 'minority culture,' the activities and ideas of Jayakar, the old revolutionary, represent the claims of 'mass culture' or of the people. The novel's distinction lies in its being able to project a balanced representation of the two, as evidenced by the articulation of the attitudes of the various characters towards India's basic problem, its crushing poverty, which is the overriding attribute of a 'backward place.' When Sudhir eloquently speaks of an elitist society and Mrs Kaul of high society and the 'bouquets' to the Prime Minister, Judy suddenly interrupts them by reminding them of the condition of the starving millions of India. Obviously Judy, in such moments, is echoing the novelist's view of India.

Among the minor characters of the novel are Etta, Clarissa, Guppy and his niece (who is, in fact, his mistress), and Mukund. Guppy is a wealthy sensual person whose philandering is mercilessly satirised. His mistress, Clarissa wants to travel abroad with him, but discovers that he has already decided to take another girl with him on his business trip.

There is no going back for Judy, who has cast her lot with Bal and with the 'backward place' where she makes her home, whatever might be the consequences. Indeed, the last scene of the novel when they are shown together travelling by train from Delhi to Bombay reflects their renewed quest for the realisation of Bal's dreams and desires.

Chapter 4 focusses on the activities of the 'Cultural Dais,' Sudhir, Mrs Kaul, Jaykar and Judy. They wish to stage a play and expect Bal to play a role in it, but he refuses saying that he will have nothing to do with it, since he has been insulted by Judy's friends. Indeed, he seems more interested in Kishan Kumar than in Mrs Kaul's theatre group. Judy speaks to Dr Hochstadt about Bal's desire to join Bombay's film world. Judy at first reacts adversely to Bal's ardent desire to move to Bombay from Delhi. Whereas Bal dreams of earning pots of money, Judy wonders whether she will ever be able to buy a carpet or at least a little rug for the room.

What follows is a portion of Chapter 4, continuing the story from this moment onwards almost to the end of the novel.

A Backward Place

Mrs Kaul threw herself into her work heart and soul. Already their first production had been decided upon, though not without a good deal of arguing to and fro among the various committee members. Several people had suggested the *Mikado*, and Mr Jumperwala had been very keen on *My Fair Lady*, and some of the others favoured either the *Shakuntala* or the *Mricchakatika* (one member, a great purist, even wanted it performed in the original Sanskrit), and one very advanced committee member, a Mrs Desai who worked with the Handloom Board, suggested the *Caucasian Chalk Circle*. Finally, however, it transpired that one among their midst, who held a well-paid executive post in an international firm and was altogether a man of the highest culture, a perceptive critic and a charming essayist, had in his student days, some twenty-five years ago, made a translation into Hindi of Ibsen's *Doll's House* which had not yet been performed. This was obviously just what they had been looking for—something original yet at the same time an attested masterpiece, a world premiere which would serve to introduce West to East and East to West. Dr Hochstadt gave it as his opinion that the *Doll's House* was particularly suitable since the social conditions in Ibsen's time might to some extent be said to correspond to social conditions in present-day India, and he brought forward some very cogent arguments to prove his point, to which they all nodded and said how true. Anyway, everyone was very pleased, except perhaps Mr Jumperwala who still cast lingering looks at *My Fair Lady* and hummed his favourite tunes from it, to show them what they were all missing.

It now only remained to get the company together and the money to finance the whole project, and while Mrs Kaul herself took over the responsibility for the latter, she delegated the former entirely to Sudhir. It was a task he took on quite cheerfully, for he knew he had only to call on Bal in whose wake would come as large a troupe of actors and other aspiring stage people as anyone could wish for.

'It's just what he's been waiting for all these years,' Judy said miserably. 'And now he says he won't.'

Sudhir said, 'Nonsense.' But he wasn't convinced it was; in fact, he thought it was rather grand of Bal not to.

'You tell him!' Judy wailed. 'You don't know how I've argued with him and quarrelled and everything, but he won't listen! He just won't! All the time he's thinking of Bombay now and his awful Kishan Kumar and when you talk to him, you might as well be talking to someone who's already there in Bombay for all he hears.'

The Doctor came in, holding in his hands a broken door latch and on his face an expression of tragedy. 'This is how my property is treated by careless tenants!'

But they had no time for him. Sudhir asked Judy, 'And he wants you to go too?'

"All of us!'

Sudhir thought about the Literacy Institute; it seemed distinctly nearer. He turned to the Doctor. 'Will you be very lonely when we've all gone away?'

The Doctor looked scornful. 'Perhaps you think you can get a better place for such rent as you are paying here? Try, only try! I invite you to try anywhere in this town!'

'Oh no, don't worry, the Cultural Dais will be with you as long as culture still flourishes. I meant Judy, if she goes.. And I...'

Judy said, 'Why you?'

'A Higher Purpose beckons.'

'Where are you two going?' the Doctor said.

'Our separate ways.' said Sudhir.

At that Judy became more downcast than ever. Everything was now—if not perfect, at least quite nearly so: the office with Sudhir in it and a regular income out of it, and a home which she liked, with Bhuaji and Shanti, and of course the children happy and well looked after. Whereas if they went, they went with and into nothing.

Sudhir also had a sinking feeling. Perhaps it was not so bad here after all; he had got used to the office, he liked Judy, he liked Jaykar, even the Doctor, all were familiar and comfortable. Nothing in the Literacy Institute would be either familiar or comfortable.

The Doctor, still holding his broken door handle, said with

a superior air, 'Yes, for you it is easy—you can run here and there, today one place, tomorrow another and the day after God knows where. It is different,' he said and rose a bit on his toes and his stomach stuck out, 'for a man of property.'

Judy looked appealingly at Sudhir. 'You talk to Bal. Tell him about the theatre group—how grand it's going to be, tell him— oh you know what. Only so he'll stay and not want to go away. So we can all stay. Oh please.'

It was never difficult to locate Bal, for all that was needed was a quick survey of one or two of the more popular coffee-houses. Sudhir found him in the midst of a group of his usual friends, all of them drinking coffee and smoking cigarettes and having, to all appearances, a nice relaxing time. When he saw Sudhir, however, Bal at once jumped to his feet to welcome him with such fervour and excitement that he knocked over his chair.

All Bal's friends looked up expectantly at Sudhir. They liked to see a new face every now and again, and perhaps get a new angle on what was going on in the world.

'Let's go somewhere else,' Sudhir said; he did not relish talking in front of so many willing ears, for one thing, nor the smell and the lazy, smoky atmosphere, for another.

'Some coffee—perhaps a cold drink—something you must have!' cried Bal, hospitably sweeping his hand round the coffee-house as if it were all his and he was putting it all at Sudhir's disposal.

But Sudhir declined everything, even to sit down, so they parted from Bal's friends and walked out together. Bal suggested going to another coffee-house, but as this too was bound to be well filled with Bal's friends, Sudhir instead took him to sit in the nearby Jantar Mantar Park. It was very pleasant there, and Bal declared himself enchanted with everything, the palm trees, the flowers, the odd astronomical shapes of the Jantar Mantar jutting up in pale grey worn stone into the azure sky.

They sat on the grass under a tree and Sudhir at once launched into the subject he had come to discuss. Such directness embarrassed Bal—who would himself have spent a long time on some polite preliminaries and only very slowly and with seeming casualness have drawn into his proper subject—and he looked shy and lowered his head and plucked blades of grass.

'It was for you we started the whole thing.' Sudhir pointed out.

'I know, oh I know. And I am so grateful.' Bal squirmed with embarrassment. If he had had adequate warning he would have known how to put his case and explain everything to his own and Sudhir's satisfaction. But caught unawares like this, he floundered.

'No one asks you to be grateful. You are only asked to become a member of the group.'

'And how much I would like to. But just now—you see, there are circumstances—' He trailed off and his attention strayed to two hoopoes pecking away at the grass.

'What circumstances?' Sudhir said.

Bal pointed at the hoopoes and said, 'What nice birds! What are they called?' He wasn't deliberately trying to change the subject, he was really interested. He spent little time outdoors, and when he did he was always charmed by all he saw.

'What circumstances?' Sudhir asked again.

'Yes,' said Bal, returning sadly to the conversation. 'You see, a friend of mine—Kishan Kumar, you must have heard of him? No? Oh he is a very famous actor, one of our leading stars.' Bal looked proud. 'And he is also very friendly to me. Kishan and I, we are so close, like brothers. Now he is starting a production unit and of course he needs me, again and again he has said Bal, please come to Bombay, please come. How can I refuse him?'

'What about Judy?'

'Of course she will come too. All of us are going.' He said this with a sort of quiet confidence, even matter-of-factness, which made it difficult to raise any protest.

Sudhir was silent for a while. Then he asked, 'You have somewhere to live there?'

Bal was not in the least troubled. He smiled: 'Oh, I have so many friends.'

'Yes, but for your wife and children—two children—'

'Of course, my friends will welcome them also,' Bal said with dignity. 'And it is only for a very short time. Then I shall take one of these new flats for them—you know, these big blocks of flats you have in Bombay, overlooking the sea. Judy will be very comfortable there,' he said with satisfaction, as if he had already installed her there.

Sudhir felt it was not his place to raise any objection. It was not as if he were a relative or had any rights over Bal and his family. And Bal was so confident, seemed so sure of himself, his plans, his future, that Sudhir felt at a disadvantage.

Nevertheless he tried again on the theatre group: 'It's quite an ambitious scheme. And of course you will be guaranteed a regular salary—'

Bal shook his head vehemently. 'For ten years—ten years!— I've been waiting here for something, and nothing has ever come. Now I'm going away. I'm going to take my own chance.'

'Yes, chance. But here it is more than chance, it is a certainty . . .' He hardly dared say more. Mrs Kaul's activities and those of her committee could not, he felt himself, be the foundation of anything certain.

Bal was not listening very carefully. Probably his mind was made up so firmly that any listening he did was only out of politeness. For the rest, he gave himself over to enjoying his surroundings. Birds sang and cawed and butterflies played in the flower-beds. The grey of old stones and the green of grass and bushes and trees were all drenched in gold by the sun. The tops of feathery palm trees tickled against a sky which was still and blue as a lake with birds floating on it, high, high up, slow and lazy.

Bal lay on the grass with his arms spread and his eyes shut blissfully and he smiled. 'How silly we are. To sit around in the coffee-house when outside it is so lovely, Sudhir,' he said.

Sudhir grunted. He felt heavy and sullen and earthbound beside Bal. Bal seemed to him like one of those birds floating on the sky—drifting without thought or effort or fear, aerial and at ease.

'How stupid I have been all these years,' Bal said with a little smile at himself. 'I should have gone away long ago. What is the use of sitting and waiting only for success to come?'

Sudhir did not answer. He was unexpectedly reminded of Jaykar, who also disapproved of sitting and waiting.

Disturbed by Sudhir's silence, Bal sat up and leaned on one elbow and said, 'Don't you think so, Sudhir? Don't you think I'm right?' He was, however, so anxious for assent and confirmation that he could not wait for Sudhir to give them but had to do so himself. 'Of course!' he cried. 'It is so, I know! Yes, I have been very stupid.' He looked thoughtful for a moment, then he lowered his voice and said confidentially, 'And I think I was afraid also to leave my home and go away. You see, I was a coward, yes a real coward,' he said in a tone which was so condemnatory that it at once inspired him to be absolutely firm with himself. 'But not any more. From now on, you will see, I shall be quite a different person. And no one will ever dare to say to me again'—and his eyes blazed dangerously—'that I can't support my own family. No one shall ever insult me like that again.'

Sudhir wondered who could have insulted Bal, but he did not

get far in this speculation, for the next moment Bal's face cleared again and he spoke out joyously—'In Bombay everything will be so different! Yes, a new life is beginning!' Then impulsively he turned to Sudhir, for he never liked anyone to be left out of anything: 'Why don't you also come with us? You can be our P.R.O.—of course we shall need one in our production unit, it is a very important assignment.' Two butterflies, chasing each other and then interlocking wing upon wing, fluttered before his face, and he put up his hand as if he meant to catch them and laughed when they eluded him. 'Sudhir, what is the use of staying always in one place?' he urged.

Etta was not surprised to find the same girl again in Guppy's suite. She had almost expected her. The girl had taken off her shoes and was lying fast asleep on Guppy's sofa. Her scarf had slipped from her bosom and was trailed half across her stomach and half across the carpet. Her bosom, thus exposed, tight, full and young in her pale green silk shirt, rose up and down as she breathed. Her cheeks were a little flushed, her mouth a little open, a few locks of dark brown hair had escaped from their pins and curled around her plump face.

'Who is she?' Clarissa whispered.

Etta smiled, part smile, part sneer. 'His niece.'

'Well we'd better call him.' Clarissa strode over to the telephone and had herself connected with Guppy's office. 'Yu-hu!' she yodelled down the line. 'Three guesses!'

Whatever his feelings might have been about this unexpected visit, he had well mastered them by the time he arrived upstairs. He came in all welcome, large and genial and rubbing his hands in simulated pleasure. His eyes just flickered over the sleeping girl, but he kept on smiling. 'Please be comfortable, quite comfortable,' he invited them. 'What shall I order for you?'

'Gin and tonic,' Clarissa said promptly.

'Excellent, excellent, very good.' He made no move to ring for a bearer though. 'Well well, you have given me a nice surprise.'

'Yes, haven't we?' said Etta, looking at the girl.

He passed it over with ease. 'It is always nice to meet with old friends. There is an Urdu saying—it goes, well I can't quite remember but it says, yes well old friends are best friends, ha-ha-ha!' He rubbed his hands again. He seemed in excellent health as well as excellent spirits. Etta thought he had put on more weight—she had always warned him about that: he really was far too fond of his food—but he was one of those people who can carry almost any amount and yet remain quick, active and light on their feet. He was dressed rather more flashily than he would have been under Etta's supervision, in suede shoes and a terylene shirt and a ring or two too many; his hair was thickly plastered with sweetly-smelling oil. Though by no means young, he appeared full of physical vigour and a not incongruous match for the girl sleeping her healthy sleep on the sofa.

Etta gave another pointed look in that direction. 'Your niece appears to be sleeping.'

'Isn't she sweet? Clarissa said, and she too looked, but in a far more kindly way. 'She's a lot like you, Guppy. Is she your brother's daughter or your sister's? You can see the family resemblance all right.' She shut one shrewd painter's eye and looked from the girl to Guppy and back again.

Etta laughed—genuinely, she was amused. Then she asked Guppy, with flippant good humour, 'What *has* she been doing to make her so tired?'

Guppy passed this over. Instead he returned to the theme of how glad he was to see them—though his cordiality was already a little cracked and gave indications of his desire to know why they had come, what they wanted, how long theywere going to stay. One foot in its suede shoe tapped up and down on the carpet.

Etta sank luxuriously into his biggest arm-chair, lit a cigarette and exhaled her first puff of smoke with an audible sigh which expressed her pleasure and satisfaction at being there and her intention to stay a good long while.

'Of course, Guppy love,' Clarissa said, 'you do know that we're tremendously happy to see you again and that we'd run one hundred thousand miles just for the pleasure of meeting you, but this time, it's no use beating about the bush, we've come with a capital P Purpose.'

'You spoil the happiest occasions,' Etta said. 'Just when he was so glad to see us for our own sakes—'

'Well I'm very sorry, I'm just no hypocrite. It's not in my temperament.' She looked at him with frank eyes. 'Now then, Guppy, we've come for money.'

He had a visible shock.

'Stick 'em up!' said Clarissa, levelling two long forefingers at him. 'Your money or your life!' She gave a laugh and lowered her fingers. 'No seriously, Gup, it's about the theatre group.'

The girl slept through everything. Wonderful, thought Etta (who never slept without the help of pills and even then could be awakened by the dropping of a pin) 'the power of youth and health. She stared at the girl as if willing her to wake up, but of course was unsuccessful: the girl went on breathing in and out, blissfully, in and out, her breath delicately fluttering the wisps of escaped hair that curled around her face. Etta looked away again disdainfully, and with the same disdainful glance, looked round the room, at the fat, shiny sofa-sets and the satin lamps, which so often she had longed to change but which she now recognized as being eminently suited not only to Guppy's personality but to the girl's as well.

'Very nice,' Guppy was saying. Etta could see that he wasn't listening very much, but Clarissa was talking ceaselessly, holding herself spellbound with her own enthusiasm. She had soon unfolded all her plans to him and he was scratching his chin with his finger-nail as was his habit when he was being cagey, though he kept saying from time to time, 'Yes, very nice, very very nice.'

Suddenly the girl gave a cry in her sleep. Everyone looked at her and expected her to wake up, but instead she tossed her heavy body to the other side and, with her back to the room, continued sleeping. Her shirt had hitched itself up and was crumpled round her waist; large round buttocks clothed in green silk stared into the room. Guppy, Etta noted, seemed embarrassed.

'I could move in whenever you say,' Clarissa said. 'And of course the sooner was start our company the better all round.' She rubbed her hands. 'You'll find me a very active campaign manager.'

'Just now we are fully booked up,' Guppy murmured.

'Oh any little old cubby-hole would do.' She began to walk round Guppy's own suite, peering into the bedroom, the bathroom, even opening a few cupboard doors.

Etta snatched at the little privacy this afforded, and asked in a low voice, 'When are you leaving?'

But Guppy, who was evidently not in the least anxious to be private with her, answered quite loudly, 'In a week or two.' To Clarissa he said, 'But this is only the linen cupboard.'

'Lovely place you have,' she said, absently opening his wardrobe.

'So you're really going.' Etta stretched out one leg (a little too white and blue-veined, but still exceedingly shapely) from her short skirt. 'And going without me.' She smiled up at him, curving her mouth in a winning way. It did not escape her notice that, almost in spite of himself, he glanced down at that provocative leg.

He cleared his throat. 'It is a business trip.' He looked round as if for distraction or rescue.

'But I mean strictly business too.' Now she stretched out the other leg as well. She didn't know what it was she was still hoping for, but she felt herself to be desperate and ready to try, dare anything. 'I'll go and book my ticket, shall I? Shall I, Gup? Say yes.' She lisped on the last ('thay yeth') and looked up at him with big, appealing, loving eyes, but at the same time her fingers tensely twisted the handle of her bag to the point of ruining it.

'A really cosy nest,' said Clarissa, returning from her tour of inspection. She clapped Guppy on the back, making the thick flesh under the terylene shirt resound. 'Snug as a bug in a rug here, aren't you.'

He didn't know what she meant, but it was obviously a great relief to him to be able to laugh. He laughed excessively, even holding his sides, to the surprise and pleasure of Clarissa, who had not expected so overwhelming a response. Etta tried to light a new cigarette, but her lighter wouldn't work, it clicked and clicked in her slightly trembling hands.

At this point the girl slowly sat up on the sofa. She was warm and flushed with sleep. She looked at them all out of brown, liquid eyes which she slowly blinked once or twice. Her scarf was still trailed half across the sofa and half across the floor. Dazed and sleepy as she was, she groped for it quickly to cover up her breasts which were very clearly in evidence through the tight silk shirt and on which, so lushly prominent were they, all eyes seemed to be fixed.

It was never any use talking about Bal to his elder brother Mukand. Mukand had given up on Bal years ago, so much so that, whenever Bal was mentioned, he would either pretend not to hear and go on reading his newspaper, or he would turn his face away and assume an expression of saintly resignation.

So Judy knew it would be no use to appeal to Mukand against Bal's decision to go away to Bombay. Mukand would want to know nothing about it, would have washed his hands of the affair before he had even touched it, though at the same time he would be, out of long habit, wearily resigned to be called upon to pull Bal out of any trouble he might with his new venture get himself into.

His wife's attitude was different. Shanti was enthusiastic about the whole idea the moment she heard about it—much to Judy's surprise and a little bit to her chagrin. She asked, 'Aren't you going to miss us?' put out to see Shanti glow and smile like that at the prospect of their departure.

Shanti had a round, middle-aged face, but her expressions were those of a young girl. As soon as Judy said that, her look of joy gave way to one of misery. 'Oh yes, it will be so dull and lonely here without you.' And then at once she changed back to joy again. 'But I'm so glad for you! It is so exciting! Bombay!' She smiled and looked dreamy and radiant. She had never travelled anywhere except, before her marriage, when she had twice visited a cousin in Dehra Doon.

Judy was amazed that Shanti could not see the terrible difficulties that she herself envisaged only too clearly. But Shanti was too enchanted by the prospect of a journey, a change of scene, for Judy and her family to be concerned with questions of where they were to live and what on.

She bent down to her youngest child, who was crawling round her feet. 'And when you grow big, you also will go to Bombay! And to Calcutta! To Dehra Doon, to Madras, to Aligarh—everywhere! To England also! Oh!' she cried and picked up the child and danced her up and down in her arms. The child's diaper had come off and she was stark naked under her little brown silk dress cut down from one of Shanti's old saris. She crowed with pleasure and put out fat little hands and grasped her mother's nose and touched her cheeks. Shanti laughed and looked into her child's face as if to read there traces of all travel and adventures in store for her.

But Judy wanted only to stay where and how she was. It wasn't a very grand place, she knew—that broken old house behind the bazaar with its flaking damp-stained walls and its dangerous electric wiring—but she had grown used to it and fond of it.

Bal nowadays was full of energy. He got up earlier than usual, whistled and sang a lot and went out to more places than ever. He was always in a good mood. Once Judy overheard him telling the children about Bombay and how they would live in a beautiful flat with a lift to go up and down, and the sea and the sea-shells and jelly-fish and whales, and their Daddy acting big parts in big films. He held his audience spellbound, and Gita and Prithvi became prouder and prouder, and how Shanti's children begged to be taken too! And the only disturbing factor was Judy, who was in the bathroom but shouted from out of there, 'No one is going!' and furiously poured water over herself out of the bucket which served them as bath.

Bal tried to ignore this interruption, and continued to entertain his listeners with fascinating stories of Bombay in general and the film world in particular. But Judy came storming out of the bathroom, still dripping wet and her sari tucked round her in very haphazard fashion, and said, 'What are you telling them all that rot for!' Bal and the children looked up at her in pained surprise.

'We're not going!' she said and stamped one foot and her wet towel slipped from off her shoulders. She snatched it up again impatiently and proceeded towards the bedroom, shaking drops of water as she went. She banged the door hard behind her. The children and Bal looked at one another.

'We're *not* going?' Gita asked him reproachfully.

'Of course,' he said. 'Of course we are.' He stroked her hair, affectionately but a little absently, looking nervously towards the closed bedroom door.

'Tell more!' Prithvi said.

Bal tried, but failed, to recapture the earlier mood. Though he dwelt on the same interesting subject, the children soon sensed that his heart was not in it, their attention wandered and soon they were off in search of other diversion. Bal timidly entered the bedroom. Judy was lying flat on the bed.

'Why do you talk like that?' he asked her.

'Because it's true. We're not going.'

He was silent.

'We're not, we're not!'

'All right,' he said quietly. He went out. She followed him at once.

'I mean it!'

'All right,' he said again.

'What do you mean—all right?'

'All right, I will go on my own.'

He went into the sitting-room and sat down on a chair and picked up a film magazine that was lying there. He didn't have time to start reading it though.

'What, and leave us here? Not on your life!'

He patiently shut the magazine and laid it aside. She watched him narrowly, as if she suspected him of intending to rush up and out of the house and off to Bombay that very moment. But he only sat quietly and modestly on his chair.

'Say something!'

'What?' he said. 'What shall I say?'

She sank down on the sofa opposite him. How hard it was!

One day they would get a real sofa, with springs.

'What do you want me to do?' he said, eyes sadly downcast.

'Stay here.' She wanted it so much, she felt, to stay here always. And one day they would have a proper sitting-room, buy proper furniture, not only a sofa but arm-chairs too and a little table with a glass top.

'And do what?' he said. 'Always the same—always running after something, hoping for something, and then it becomes nothing.'

This was perhaps the first time he had ever looked at his activities of the last ten years so squarely. Also it was probably the first time she had heard him speak of his life with any degree of bitterness. But she was at that moment too taken up with her own feelings to pay much attention to his. She was flooded with love for the shabby little room in which they sat and which was theirs. She looked with sentimental eyes at his two framed certificates and his photograph at the airport, and promised all three of them a grand future in silver frames.

'There is nothing here for me,' Bal said.

'The theatre group will be starting soon.'

'Don't talk to me of your theatre group! I want nothing to do with it. I want nothing to do with any of your precious friends.'

'Silly,' she said, quite affectionately. She would buy vases too and a lot of little ornaments. She was sorry for a moment that there was no mantelpiece in the room.

'Judy, but in Bombay—ah, you will see! How happy you will be there! And you will be so proud to speak of me to your friends and tell them now he is acting in this picture, now in that picture, he is earning lakhs and lakhs of rupees. Lakhs and lakhs!' he cried and laughed out loud and came over to her and embraced her with enthusiasm.

She pushed him away. Perhaps even a carpet on the floor, she

A Backward Place

thought; or at least a little rug.

Mrs Kaul did not slacken in her efforts. A woman of energy and ambition, once she had fastened on to a scheme she did not let go till she had pushed it through to its limits. Or rather, to *her* limits: for though she did manage, by persistence and ambition, to get a thing on to its feet, it somehow never grew or prospered to any thing more than she and her friends could conceive of. Their ambitions were large but their conceptions—based as they were not so much on any profound inner need as on something heard or read about and found desirable—were so vague and weak that everything that came of them also tended to be vague and weak. That was what had happened with the Cultural Dais as well as with one or two previous schemes (such as a Discussion Group and an International Music Circle): finally everything turned out disappointing, and then Mrs Kaul had to look for something new.

The theatre group came just in time to save her from the disappointment the Cultural Dais was turning out to be. She threw herself into it with enthusiasm. Once she summoned Sudhir urgently to her house and, when he got there, he found her in an elated state. She sat in her drawing-room, drinking tea out of a transparent china cup and told him with an air of triumph, 'We are making very good progress!'

'Oh?' said Sudhir, who had thought they weren't making any.

She dropped several lumps of sugar into her tea with a pair or silver tongs. 'I'm getting so many actors together. It is surprising how much talent there is.'

Sudhir wondered whether she had got on to Bal and his companions. He was surprised. He hadn't thought there was any direct road that could connect Mrs Kaul and Bal.

'It all happened yesterday at a dinner the Mahajans gave for the Swedish Ambassador.' She smiled. 'Mrs Mahajan confessed to me that in her college days she took a great interest in dramatics. Then we discovered there were so many other friends who had a lot of acting experience—Mrs Moitra, the wife of our Principal Secretary, had taken part in many fine performances while she was studying at Shantiniketan, and Mrs Labh Singh— the Major-General's wife—had taken a leading role in a regimental performance of *Arsenic and Old Lace* when they were stationed at Simla. And we all remembered that young Captain Lakshman was a leading light in the Army Headquarters Dramatic Group and—oh, we discovered so much talent!' she cried gaily, terribly pleased with herself, her friends and last night's party. Then she leaned forward and confided to Sudhir, 'It is best to keep it all as much as possible among people we know.'

Sudhir drew back instinctively as if wishing to dissociate himself completely from people one knew.

'One great advantage also, these people won't be greedy for money like those other actors, on the contrary, they will be very happy to give their services free of charge. They are all deeply interested in the advancement of the theatre movement in our country.'

Sudhir came to a sudden decision. 'I shall be leaving soon. I'm going to Madhya Pradesh.'

Mrs Kaul put down her tea-cup. She dabbed an embroidered napkin against her upper lip. 'I'm afraid it will be difficult for you to take leave just now. The burden of work will be very heavy while we are establishing our group.'

'I'm not taking leave,' Sudhir said brusquely. 'I'm leaving.'

Mrs Kaul accepted this in pained silence. She stared in front of her, at a Chinese silk hanging on the wall (brought back by Mr Kaul from a mission in Peking).

'I'm going to teach in a Literacy Institute. I think my level of culture doesn't really rise higher than to neo-literates.'

'Just at this time,' Mrs Kaul said in a voice trembling with reproach.

'But you don't need me! When you have Mrs Mahajan and Captain—what was his name? who can all afford to donate their talents free of charge.'

'We have worked together side by side.' He noticed that she was really hurt, and it embarrassed him. 'And now, just when our biggest effort of all is beginning... I thought the work meant so much to you.'

Sudhir didn't even feel tempted to tell her just what it meant to him. He had often pleasurably anticipated the moment when he would be handing in his resignation and had never expected the occasion to turn out, the way it was now doing, in any way painful for him.

And then she was quite different. She cried out in a voice rich in real feeling, 'It means so much to me! Without this work, what is there in my life?'

He wished she would stop, but saw that there was little chance of that now. He took off his glasses and cleaned them and put them on, and then he took them off and cleaned them again. He knew exactly what she would say, and that was what she did say. Mr Kaul all day in his office, and always committees and meetings and not a moment to spare for her; and the children away at boarding-school (naturally, one wanted only the best for one's children)—who was there for her? Who needed her? She sat here in this big house, perhaps people envied her, but—ah, if they only knew, if they could only read into her heart.

She took a sip of tea for comfort, and when she had done so, she said, 'I'm like a bird in a gilded cage.' He realized by the way the phrase came out so patly that she had used it before and more than once, perhaps when she had sat like this in her drawing-room, drinking tea with some lady friend, and had suddenly been overcome by the feeling that life had not offered her everything it seemed once to have promised.

Etta phoned Guppy every day, and sometimes she went to see him. He was always cordial with her, both over the telephone and when they met, but at the same time brisk and preoccupied so that it was difficult to speak about anything very personal. Etta tried all sorts of angles but he was too adroit for her. When she became serious, he contrived to call one of his staff and became involved in giving instructions. Once or twice the girl was there, and Guppy did not tell her to go away, and she sat there, lush and passive, pervading the room with her physical attributes, so that it was difficult to concentrate on anything but her.

These were bad days for Etta. She stayed at home most of the time, and sometimes she did not even bother to get dressed but lay on her unmade bed all day. She ate almost nothing but smoked an exorbitant number of cigarettes.

For the first time she disliked her flat, though she had taken so much trouble with it and had made it as chic and modern as she still knew how. Now it was stale with cigarette smoke, untidy and dusty, closed in like a cage. Yet it was a cage that was necessary to her and out of which she would not break even if she could: for outside lay the dusty landscape, the hot sun, the vultures, the hovels and shacks and the people in rags that lived there till some dirty disease carried them off.

She lay on her bed and smoked and thought about Europe. It was infinitely distant and infinitely desirable. But she was afraid of it too. Here at least she had her personality: she was Etta, whom people knew and admired for being blonde and vivacious and smart. In Europe there were many blondes, and there they might more easily notice that she was not as young or as vivacious as she once had been; and they might not think her smart at all.

She no longer knew the way they dressed there, or the way they talked, or the fashionable foods they ate and drinks they drank, the books they had read, the conversations they had held with one another, while she was out here.

Yet if she could have gone with Guppy, it would have been all right. She would have been rich, protected, staying in the best hotels. She would have carried everything off beautifully and been treated with deference by waiters, taxi-drivers, hairdressers and shop assistants. But on her own there would be nothing like that. Instead she would be arriving with her smart suitcases and there would be nowhere to go, no one to meet her, no one to know who she was. She could not face it: to break through such a barrier of indifference would take more strength and youth than she had had for a good number of years. She longed for Europe, it was true, and would do anything to get there, but she could no longer tackle it on her own.

Once Judy came to see her. Etta raised her head from her pillow, took in Judy wearing a sari and her hair in a bun, groaned 'You look awful,' and then wearily sank back again.

Judy tried to hide it, but she was shocked by Etta's appearance. She had never seen her like this. Etta's face looked sunken and the skin stretched tight over the fine bone structure; there was something about her eyes and forehead which made it seem as if she had been suffering from a severe headache for a long time. She looked strained and—thought Judy hardly liked to think it even to herself—old.

'Why've you come?' Etta asked with her eyes shut. 'Don't you know I've had a fearful row with your precious what's-his-name? Where's your wifely loyalty?'

Judy hadn't meant to bring up this subject at all, and now that it had been, she wanted only to pass it over. She didn't feel she had any quarrel with Etta. She was sorry, of course, that she and Bal should have had such a scene but wasn't inclined to blame either of them. It was all, she was sure, some awful misunderstanding. Bal and Etta were unfortunately two people made to misunderstand one another.

'He wants to take us to Bombay.' she said. She got ready to tell Etta the whole story but Etta cried, 'I don't want to hear! I'm just not interested!'

Judy did not insist. She got up and walked round the flat. She noticed that everything looked different. There was a layer of dust and ashtrays were full to overflowing. The windows were all shut and the curtains drawn over them.

'Where's your servant?' Judy aksed. She suspected that Etta had dismissed him—she changed servants frequently—and hadn't got a new one yet. She wanted to offer to tidy up a bit, and perhaps get Etta something to eat; it seemed to her that Etta was sick, and she was sad to see her so alone.

'Oh he's around somewhere,' Etta said. 'I've told him not to come in here—I can't stand him around, I simply cannot. He smells so.' After a moment she added, 'They all smell.' She hated servants. They perspired and wore dirty clothes and were stupid and dishonest.

Judy hesitantly picked up one of the full ashtrays. 'Shall I—'
'No! Put it down! Don't touch anything! Don't *fuss*!'

Judy quickly put it down again' She stood by Etta's bedside, awkwardly findling with the loose end of her sari. She felt she ought to do something but didn't know what. 'Are you sick?' she said at last, in a cracked, uncertain voice.

'Yes I am. Sick, sick, sick. Sick to the depths of my soul.'

'Oh dear.' This mild comment was not made to be ironic, but it was the only one that rose readily to Judy's lips. After it had crossed them, she stood and bit them.

Etta painfully screwed her face into an expression of disgust.

'Your sympathy overwhelms me.' Then she turned her face to the wall. 'Oh go away,' she said.

Judy stood there twiddling her sari a while longer. Etta didn't stir, pretending to be asleep. 'I'll be going then,' Judy offered. This brought no response. 'Goodbye' Judy said standing still.

She waited in vain. So she left the bedroom and went into the next room to reach the main door. She walked reluctantly. She had already opened the door and was about to close it quietly behind her when the summons she had been waiting for came. At once she was back by Etta's bedside. 'Did you call?'

Etta said wearily: 'I'll probably be going away soon.'

'Oh, Etta.'

That seemed to sting her. She sat up. Her blonde hair, which now looked very brittle and false, slipped down over her face and she pushed it back impatiently. 'You think I'm here for ever? You think I'm going to let myself *rot* in this—this—'

'Hole,' Judy tactfully suggested.

'Hell!' Etta emended with violence. 'No, thank you, I rather flatter myself I've been reserved for a better fate. I'm packing up. I'm getting out.' She swung herself off the bed as if she meant to there and then. She paced the room angrily, her arms folded, holding a cigarette between the fingers of one veined, nervous hand. She was wearing her nylon apricot-coloured negligee, but it was somewhat crushed. She had no fresh make-up on and traces of the old had remained on her face, making it look discoloured; her lips were thin and very pale and her eyes dim. It pained Judy to find her so unglamorous.

'It may be all right for you here,' Etta said. 'God knows why, but you don't seem to care how you live or where or with what sort of people. But I care! Passionately!' She took a long pull from her cigarette and filled her lungs with smoke in a deep, passionate breath. 'I've wasted quite enough of my life here. Now it's for

me to get back where I belong. To a civilized place.' She looked
Judy up and down as she stood there in her crumpled cotton sari.
'The trouble with you is you've forgotten what it's like to be civilized. To wear decent clothes—go to theatres—concerts—drink
wine with meals—' She brought up her clasped hands to her forehead and shut her eyes and seemed rapt beyond speech with long-
ing and desire.

Judy saw that Etta was moved by strong feelings, so she sym-
pathized with her. But for herself she had none of these feelings.
The things Etta spoke of were familiar to Judy only from the
magazines and the pictures, and she had no hopes that they would
ever enter into her own circumstances. Her Western world was
only little semi-detacheds with smoking fires and frozen pipes
and carefully drawn curtains bought at two and eleven a yard at
the sales.

When Etta had recovered sufficiently, she at once renewed her
attack on Judy. 'I don't know how, but somehow or other you've
managed to fool yourself you actually *like* being here.' And quickly she forestalled the protest which Judy in any case wasn't going
to make. 'Don't try and fool me, though! Making a virtue out of
necessity may be a favourite English pastime, but no one asks
you to pretend you find it a pleasurable exercise. My dear child,
I wasn't born yesterday. I can *see* what's happening to you. Look
at you, just look at you!'—and this was said so peremptorily that
Judy really looked at herself in the mirror, but saw nothing very
extraordinary.

Suddenly Etta came up behind her and pulled the pins out of
her hair. Judy's hair, which she did up in a plain bun (in order to
look like everybody else—Shanti, Bhuaji and all the neighbouring
women) came falling down over her shoulders. It was fair, very fine
hair. And with another tug Etta pulled off the sari, so that it dropped off and lay in a pool round Judy's feet. There was Judy in

A Backward Place

her sari-petticoat and the short blouse, looking young and vigorous and pleasing, with her apple breasts, her bright blue eyes and her fair hair framing her face.

Judy blushed. Her face—too pale after ten years in India—was suddenly the fresh pink it had been intended for. At that moment Etta, who, fearing perspiration, human dirt, alien flesh, usually hated touching anyone, put an arm round her and said, 'Come on, we'll go together, you and I—we'll take a place somewhere, in England, France, Italy, anywhere you like, and we'll have a good time! Shall we, Judy, shall we?'

Judy was embarrassed. First, by Etta touching her, which was unexpected, and then too by something desperate in Etta's tone which she could not understand. To hide her embarrassment, she stooped to pick up her sari and tuck it back into her petticoat-string.

Etta turned away form her. She stubbed out her cigarette and lit a new one. After a time she said, 'Catch me going anywhere you!'—and she laughed in a dry, hard way. Judy uneasily laughed with her.

(From *A Backward Place*, Hind Pocket Books, New Delhi)

4. MANOHAR MALGONKAR

Manohar Malgonkar was born in an aristocratic family in Bombay in 1913. His grandfather was Diwan (Chief Minister) in the erstwhile Maratha state of Indore in Central India. At the age of ten, Manohar Malgonkar took to hunting and developed a love for forests. He was a professional shikari before he joined the Indian Army, in which he rose to the rank of a Lieutenant Colonel. He took part in the Burma War and his first novel *Distant Drum* (1961) was based on his experiences of this war. After leaving the army he was for some time a teaplanter in southern India—an experience which gave him material for his second novel, *Combat of Shadows* (1962). Thus, of all the Indo-Anglian writers, Malyonkar has had the most varied experience of the Indian milieu. He contested, though unsuccessfully, two Parliamentary elections. He now lives at Jagalbet, a village in Belgaum district.

Malgonkar's personal involvement with the Indian princes—deep and serious as it has been—is visible in his two studies of Maratha history: the *Puars of Dewas Senior* (1963) and *The Chhatrapatis of Kolhapur* (1971). It is even more noticeable in his novel *The Princes* (1963), which was highly commended by E.M. Forster. His other fictional works are *A Bend in the Ganges* (1964), *Spy in Amber* (1971) and *The Devil's Wind* (1972). In addition he has written several volumes of short stories.

As a writer of fiction, Malgonkar has shown himself to be a competent craftsman, although not all his works can be regarded as virtuoso performances. His style is marked by urbanity, grace, lucidity and precision. His themes are varied and significant and indicate the extraordinary range of his knowledge of the Indian scene. He is, however, not an innovator, either of form or technique. He is an excellent story-teller but rather conventional in technique, following as he does, the models suggested by novelists like Rudyard Kipling and Meadows Taylor.

The Princes is a story of the Indian princely order (told as it were by an 'insider') with two fully realised characters: Hiroji, the Maharajah of Begwad state, and his son, Abhayaraj, who is also the narrator. It seems at once an epic of feudal Indian aristocracy and an autobiography of Abhayraj, the young hero. Historically, it catches the personal predicaments of the Indian rulers and the political ferment of the Indian states on the eve of their abolition as independent political entities. Poli-

The Princes

tical unrest in Begwad began around 1938 and continued till its merger in 1949 into a union of states. This movement towards merger was an inexorable historical process, a political movement which swept the whole country. Individuals, specially the rulers of states and their associates, were swept away by this tide of events, and the novel explores their fate. Maharajah Hiroji could not come to terms with the new world which had no use for the values of the old aristocracy. He goes in search of a wounded tiger and is killed by the animal—an apparent suicide in the eyes of those who knew him. Abhayraj, however, comes to accept the change signalled by the historical developments, surrenders his titles and privileges, although in his scale of values he is close to his father Hiroji.

The Princes traces Abhayraj's growth as an individual from childhood through adolescence to adulthood. He matures into manhood through several experiences of war and sex. His affair with Minnie ends in frustration when she is married to an army man called Punch. She, however, plays a role in the story of his growth and maturity. He finally marries Kamala, who stands by him in his hour of crisis as Minnie could never have done.

Abhayraj is also inexorably involved in the ramifications of the private lives of his parents. His attitude to his mother, the Maharani, whom his father had often treated as a chattel, is curiously ambivalent. She is a totally neglected woman. She falls in love with Abdulla Jan, a palace employee, marries him, changes her religion and decides to settle down with him in Karachi. Abhay, who realises the sorrows of his mother, disapproves of her betrayal of the princely tradition of Begwad. Meanwhile, Kanakchand, the son of a cobbler, becomes the President of the Praja Mandal and leads demonstrations against the ruler he had once served.

Abhayraj enjoys the power of the throne for only forty-nine days. The irony of his situation is that the moment of his commitment to his father's values is also the moment of his abdication of power. He is no longer the detached spectator, but a participant in the pathetic drama of Begwad. *What follows is the description of the tiger hunt and Maharajah Hiroji's death (chapter 29) and the touching scene of the meeting between Abhayraj and his mother (chapter 30):*

The Princes

"IN THAT I SHALL REJOICE"

I sat for the tiger beat as I had sat for a dozen other tiger beats, wholly captivated by the atmosphere and trying to keep my mind from wandering. I sat alone with my thoughts, in a cage of green leaves high up on a platform in a tree, listening to the weird music of the beat that had suddenly replaced the frightened stillness of the jungle: coo-ees and catcalls, the curt, nervous yells of har-har-har, the snatches of song, the sounds of coughing—the indescribable, unmistakable concert of shikar.

Then the sudden break in the pattern of sound, a new theme introduced by a gentle, barely audible, tap-tap-tap of wood on wood somewhere close on my right, setting up an almost unbearable rush of blood through my veins and quickening my heartbeats. It was a signal telling a definite story. It meant that the tiger had been sighted by one of the stops on my right, that any moment now, he would emerge before me.

I had never wanted a machaan to myself. All the same I found myself being caught up in the drama of the hunt, this most prized hunt of India, the tiger beat, in which the art and science and the cunning of man combine to kill the noblest and handsomest of all beings in creation.

You take your seat on one of the artfully camouflaged platforms called the machaans that are put up in the trees, and wait in the brooding silence of the jungle for the beat to start. You are the 'gun'—the hunter. On both sides of the guns are the 'stops' also sitting up in trees, and it is their business to guide the tiger to the guns. Then comes the signal, the shrill sounding of the horn for the drive to begin, and the thin line of men waiting a mile or so away begins to creep forward, keeping within sight of each other, and yelling all the while

The Princes

to drive the tiger to the hunters. The whole thing is something like putting a wayward bull into a pen, only it is intended to bring a tiger to its death.

Was it murder? I have often asked myself this. Perhaps it was. And yet I am convinced that a hunter has not really lived unless he has sat up for a tiger in a beat.

And this was a special beat for a very special tiger, the hundredth tiger of a man who was going to be fifty. And even if he was not going to be the biggest tiger anyone had ever shot, we were quite safe in assuming that he would find a place in the book of records.

My father's machaan was on my left. The tiger was coming from the right, which meant that he would come to my machaan. I cursed the fates. Was his nasib going to deny him this last niggardly favour? I felt a twinge of anger at the perversity of things. Why should I meekly accept what was denied to him? Could I not act as a 'stop' myself and by making a slight noise guide the tiger to my left, so that my father could get a shot?

There was a rustle in the bamboos which faced me, and then I could see the orange head, enormous and bearded, staring at me from hardly thirty yards away. I did not know how long he had been there before I saw him. Even though I had seen him before, his bigness made me catch my breath. I could see only the head, peering at me through the bamboos, and I had my sights trained on it. I could have shot him clean through the head at that range. But I waited for that last split second of indecision. Should I take him or send him away?

My heart stopped thumping, and I knew that I was nervous no longer but cool and deliberate. I held the 450/400 by Healy and Lock, pressed firmly into my shoulder, the safety-catch pushed forward, finger on the trigger.

It was the tiger who made up my mind for me. Some movement behind him made him start and leap forward—a great, springy bound that caught me off balance—and then he began to go off in a quick run, head held low, stomach to the ground, a vivid flash of orange through the waist-high green of the wild turmeric. Once again he was breaking out of the beat. I swung the barrels with him, held the bead just ahead of the front leg and squeezed off.

He gave a short, curt roar and bounded high into the air with the shot and fell on his side, thrashing out with all four legs, and my second shot clean missed him and crashed into the bamboos. As I was loading again, he managed to get to his feet and went bounding away out of sight into the dense matted jungle behind my machaan.

According to custom, we stopped the beat from coming on and warned everyone to climb up a tree, for now there was the danger of a wounded tiger attacking anyone who came close. Within a few minutes, my father and Hanuman Singh came up to my machaan and all of us went and examined the ground where the tiger had been when he was hit.

A good deal of thin, light-red blood had splashed on the leaves and grass where he had fallen and a trail of blood showed the direction he had taken. Hanuman Singh followed the trail for a few yards and brought my father some leaves with blood on them.

'He has been hit quite badly, Your Highness,' said Hanuman Singh. 'More in the stomach than in the chest,' he pronounced. 'The bullet has gone clean through.'

My father examined the leaf with almost professional detachment. 'Yes, in the belly,' he said. 'What about the other one'?

'The second shot was a miss, Your Highness,' Hanuman Singh said. It has made a clean furrow in the ground and then rebounded into the bamboos.'

I knew I had missed my second shot, but I had not realized that my first one had caught him so far back.

'Must have been running quite fast,' my father said.

'Well, he was fast,' I told him.

'Did you have a good look? Is it really the giant?'

'Yes, Dada,' I said, there can be no mistaking him.'

'We will give him half an hour,' my father said, looking at his watch. 'By that time, if he's got it bad, he'll be too stiff to do any damage. If he hasn't then we owe it to him to finish him off.'

The general rules were that a wounded tiger had to be tracked and finished off, but you could give it half an hour so that it would stiffen wherever it might be lying up. After that, you went and finished it off. You sought the tiger out and killed it, not so much because it was going to be a danger to the villagers or to show how very brave you were, but because you owed it to the tiger not to leave it in pain.

There were local variations to the rules concerning the business of finishing off a wounded tiger. The safest method was to put a herd of buffaloes in the patch of jungle where the animal had disappeared and follow them. The buffaloes would scent out the tiger and become restless when they came close: then the tiger would usually attack the nearest buffalo, giving the hunter a good opportunity to shoot it. In some places it was up to the hunter himself to finish his tiger. He could take a professional tracker with him to follow the blood trail and lead him up to the tiger, but it was his business t keep the tracker covered.

Our local rule happened to be that it was the privilege of the host, my father, to go after all wounded tigers.

We talked in subdued voices at the foot of my machaan. The sudden return of silence to the jungle after the cacophony of the beat was oppressive. The bearers brought out oversized thermoses of tea and arranged orange-coloured bakelite plates and yellow and blue tea-cups on a canvas sheet spread on the ground. We sat down and sipped the tea and munched the biscuits mechanically. I had a felling that Hanuman Singh was avoiding looking at me.

Both Hanuman Singh and myself knew perfectly well that it was no use trying to prevent my father from going after the tiger, but we both pleaded to be allowed to go with him.

'It is a one-man job,' Father explained. 'Two might botch it, and three is quite dangerous. Only when the shikari is not himself able to do the tracking, can he take another man with him, but then it always adds to the risk. When the man with the gun is also the tracker, it is absolutely fool-proof—as you know.'

We did know. He was not showing off, but stating a fact. He had always gone after wounded tigers alone, and he had always managed to get them, unless of course, they were too lightly wounded and had escaped. If they were lying in wait they were as good as dead. There was no denying the fact that with him doing both the tracking and the shooting, it was absolutely fool-proof as he had said.

And if he went after wounded tigers you did not feel that he was flaunting his courage, but that it was because he knew how dangerous the game was and knew that he could do what had to be done better than anyone else. He was that rare combination, both the mark man and the shikari, the man who could drop a running black-buck at three hundred yards and who could also tell the age and sex of a bison by a hazy hoof-mark in the dust and judge the span of the horns within a couple of inches. He was not just a man who had made a habit of shooting down falling coins to soothe his ruffled nerves; he could tell by the track of a snake whether it was poisonous or harmless, could call up a tiger by answering its roars, making them a challenge or a mating call according to its mood; he could even call up a jungle cock by clucking like a hen. He could read a game-trail better than his most experienced shikaris; a blood-drop, a bent leaf, the droppings of animals, a blade of grass springing back into shape, were like signposts to him.

My father was the only one who helped himself to two slices of chocolate cake and asked for a second cup of tea. Then we all lit cigarettes again. By the time I had finished mine, I knew that the half-hour must be drawing to a close, but I did not want to look at my watch.

Father crushed his cigarette into the ground and stood up. 'Well, that's the half-hour,' he said.

He broke his rifle, the big .465 double by Rigby, inserted two cartridges into the chambers and snapped the barrels home. There were four more cartridges in the loops of his jacket and perhaps another half dozen in his pockets. He tucked his rifle under his arm and walked away, without a word as always, quick and slim and erect, the cool professional who had so nearly reached his century of tigers, trim and business-like in his jungle-green golfing cap and his gaberdine bush-jacket with its pattern of leaves.

Just before he disappeared into the bamboos, he turned and waved to me. Then he was gone.

There was the usual feeling of something pressing tightly down in my chest, and my fingers as I lit a fresh cigarette were like ice. It was long afterwards, when I had finished the cigarette and thrown away the butt, that it suddenly struck me that all those other times I had seen him go after a tiger he had never paused to look back and wave. I was about to remark on this to Hanuman Singh when we heard the quick, coughing, grunting roar of a tiger's charge, like canvas tearing or a saw biting into hard wood.

Hanuman Singh and I looked at each other for a second of eternity, keyed up to hear the roar of my father's rifle, and then, without a word, we grabbed our rifles and ran into the jungle.

There was a film of sweat running over my eyes—or were they tears?—and I could not see very much as I went running forward in the hunter's crouch, tearing through thorns, wild turmeric and bamboos, blindly following Hanuman Singh's back, keeping close behind him. We had hardly gone a couple of hundred yards when I saw him drop on one knee and bring his rifle to his shoulder.

The magnificent orange and black head with the orb of snow-white beard was there again, rising as though out of the earth, coming towards us with a spellbinding slowness, as in a dream, and there was that deadly sound of the quick, tortured grunt. I saw the muzzle of Hanuman Singh's rifle lift in recoil and heard the roar of the shell going off. And then I was firing my own Healy and Lock, both barrels hitting true and solid into the orange mass of shoulder and head from hardly twenty yards away. The tiger stopped rising, stopped without ever beginning the spring that he was preparing for and fell back and lay with his great white forelegs stretching straight out in a patch of spurting blood, side by side with the body of my father.

We dashed forward, not even bothering to make sure that the tiger wa really dead. But before we came to where they were lying, I found Hanuman Singh's hand holding me back and turning me round, and he stood blocking my path with his body, shielding me from the sight.

'Don't go on; you must not look,' he told me.

I brushed away his hand and pushed him aside. I wanted to look. This was my show more than his, and I did not want to shirk the punishment. I wanted to see for myself how my father had met his death, he who now lay there with his face mangled out of recognition, his shooting jacket limp and shapeless and wet with blood and covered with a mess of oozing intestines.

I picked up the rifle which lay close to him. The barrels were clean and blue and shiny. I broke the rifle. It was just as I had thought. There were no cartridges in the chambers. He must have extracted them as soon as he was out of our sight.

Hanuman Singh took off his own jacket and covered my father's body, while I busied myself with the details of the rifle. I pulled out two cartridges from the loops in his jacket. The blood still felt warm on them. I wiped them clean with my handkerchief and inserted them into his rifle. I put the rifle to my shoulder and fired both shots in the sky. I did not want anyone other than Hanuman Singh to know that the Maharaja of Begwad had committed suicide because he had made up his mind not to sign the document of merger. I did not want to give his enemie a chance to speculate whether it was an act of bravery or of cowardice on his part to have taken that way out.

'Come, Your Highness,' Hanuman Singh said very gently. 'I think we have done whatever is necessary.'

And it did not seem odd to me that he had addressed me as 'Your Highness.'

We did not measure the tiger. I did not want him to be stretched and pulled about and humbled, his pink, de-skinned carcass left for a feast of vultures. In my mind, he was no longer a tiger but something of a divine instrument sent to aid my father in his hour of need, something that had made it possible for him to realise his wish that he would not like to see the end, made it possible, too, for him to die in the way he would have wished.

I gave instructions for the tiger to be cremated where he lay, in a high pile of sandalwood. The giant of Kolaras did not go into a book of records, but he had suddenly become something of a god.

I GO AS I CAME

I was ruler of Begwad for exactly forty-nine days. As soon as the customary thirteen days of mourning had passed, there was the ritual of my ascending the gadi of the Bedars, all quite ridiculous since I was going to have to abdicate within a few weeks. But this was what everyone seemed to want, and I submitted without protest. At the accession durbar, I was duly proclaimed by the court heralds to be Valorous as the sun, the Chosen of Ambica, the Source of all light, Wazir-e-farzand, Intezem-e-daulat, Sar-e-sarband, Prithwi-naresh, Sena-dhurandar, who held undisputed sway over the territory from the Kali to the Nashi, His Highness the Maharaja of Begwad Abhayraj Bedar III.

For forty-nine days I was all that, but I expect it was too short a time to give me the feeling that I was above all men. There were too many things to do, most of them unpleasant, and there was so little time to do them in.

On the 25 February Begwad was to be merged in the Union of Padmakoshal, which was to be formed by joining up four 'A' class states, Tilkatta, Begwad, Aweda and Ninnore, and eleven 'B' class states. The capital of the new union was to be Begwad. The administration was to be in the hands of a council of seven ministers, one each from the four 'A' class states and three in all from the 'B' class states. Kanakchand Gaur was the unopposed choice from Begwad. Indeed, for a time it was believed that he would become the Chief Minister, but towards the end there was a rift among the Mandal leaders and he was made the Education Minister.

As I said, I had much to do in the time at my disposal. I carried out a tour of the entire state, stopping at every single village, and tried to explain to the people what was happening. Wherever I went, I had to answer the same round of questions. Yes, the state was going to be finished off within a few days, I told them. There was no use mincing words. I had myself got used to the idea of merger, but sometimes, when I saw tears in the eyes of some of the people who had come to greet me, I used to be caught up in their emotions. I did not tell them it was all for their own good, because I have never really believed that it was. For my part, I felt sorry for them because they had not been consulted and were being passed over from one authority to another without any attempt to ascertain their wishes.

I had no solutions to offer, only soft words and I would not have cared whether they received me with black-flag demonstrations or garlands. But there were no black-flag demonstrations. On the other hand, I was overwhelmed by their kindness and enthusiasm, and the things they said about my father. They were awed and bewildered by the future. The changes were too abrupt and too drastic for their comprehension. What they could see and feel for was the break from the past, knowing that they were being torn away from something they had not just learnt to live with but had begun to value.

My task was particularly difficult and exasperating in the Bulwara district, for here were the people I had been brought up to regard as my own. I had a special obligation towards them because they were almost childlike in their ignorance and also in their range of emotions. They had known no other master than the Bedar, and he too had been only half a king to them because he was also their god. They were like animals caught up in a game-drive, bewildered and suspicious, conscious of being led where they had no intention of going.

Yes, the Bulwara dam was going up, I told them, but they must understand how it was going to benefit the rest of the country, harnessing an immense amount of electricity and bringing water to dry lands hundreds of miles away.

They would shake their heads and look at me sullenly. Then their leaders would begin to argue. 'Yes, but our own land will be going under water, they say to the depth of seven bamboos. We neither want canal water nor bijli-batti. Why should we be made to give up what is ours for the sake of those who live hundreds of miles away? Was it for the Marwaries to make lakhs of rupees by running mills and factories? Even the topiwalla sarkar, the British, gave in when we protested.'

In a way I could understand their bitterness, for they stood to lose everything that was dear to them, their lands and their homes which had been saved for them from the British by their Maharaja. I, their new Maharaja, could do nothing for them.

I gave them what answers I could, feeling the inadequacy of

my explanations, wondering if I had the necessary hold on their affection to make them believe that whatever was happening was for their own good merely because I was telling them it was so. I told them that they were bound to get a fair compensation for their lands and houses and possibly even alternative holdings.

They would nod their heads as though they understood, and for a time they would remain quiet. Then they would start whispering amongst themselves and come right back to the beginning. Was there no way of resisting? Why not make protest marches against the Residency as they had planned to do when the British had threatened to put their land under water? Could they not resist with force? Should they not go on sit-down strikes, refusing to leave their home-steads as Dada-maharaja had advised them to do?

No, no, no! My head would begin to spin, and I had to remind myself to be patient, knowing that it would never do to lose my temper with them.

'Remember that what you are going to lose is going to be a gain a thousand times over to the country.'

'What country? The Bedar's state'?

And again, no.

'It is that Dhor-babu's doing, the Dhor is the villain. We will burn his effigy, we will set the churail to haunt his sleep. We are not going to let him enter our district. That was Dada maharaja's wish.'

'No,' that was not Dada-maharaja's wish. He had changed his mind lately, as you know from the advice he gave your leaders before going to Delhi. He told you to call off your agitation, remember? Things have changed, you do not realize. Kanakchand is going to be a big man ... a Minister ... possibly the Chief Minister, with more power even than the Maharaja had. He could do much harm. Don't give him cause for offence. There is the question of compensation for your lands. How much you get will depend on how you behave towards him now. . . .'

'Oh, we are not afraid of that bit of dirt and his men—eunuchs who ran away from us. We are only afraid of what you will say. We were sure that Dada-maharaja would never have got angry with us. . .we are not sure of you. If you tell us to resist, we will resist; we are not afraid. We were not afraid of the sahibs, and we will not be afraid of ten governments! Let them kill us before they take away what has always been ours. . . .'

I did not know how my father would have handled this situation, and the thought went fleeting through my brain that he had perhaps taken the easier way out. We talked in circles, late into the night, and in the end I could only appeal to their loyalty; I told them they had to accept the coming of the dam as a personal favour to me, that they were not to offer any resistance if only to hold up the honour of the Bedars in the eyes of the world.

I said my farewell to them with my head still in a whirl, not at all sure that I had been able to convince them, distressed by the knowledge that they would have to suffer much before they could be brought to accept the inevitable.

The next afternoon I visited the Patalpat fort, right down on the floor of the valley, hugging the sheer wall of the mountain on one side and with the river making a loop on three sides. There I had to face the issues squarely all over again.

I had heard the voice before, but I had not seen the face. Now he stood before me, tall and wiry, in a costume that was a relic from some indeterminate past, his beard a metallic white, his eyes bits of coal, his face a teak mask. He was the head of the Ramoshi clan, the hereditary guardians of the fort.

'There is talk of the whole valley being put under water to the depth of seven bamboos. Surely that is not true'? he asked.

I told him it was true.

'Who can flood the Bedar's fort in the Bedar's land'?

He was still in the middle of the eighteenth century. I explained as simply as I could how neither the fort nor the valley belonged to the Bedars any more. 'It belongs to the people,' I ended up. 'Not to any ruler. It belongs to all of you.'

'All of us don't want the dam to come.'

'It belongs to the Government, then; the sarkar from Delhi wants it.'

'The white badshah from Bilayat'? he asked.

'No, the King from Bilayat is gone. We have our own king now.'

'Has the Mughal Badshah come back'?

'No, it is the people's raj, the people are the Badshah. Neither the Mughals nor the British, but the people...you.'

He cocked his head slightly and looked at me morosely, just like a dog who does not understand what it has done wrong.

'Then what happens to what is in the fort?—the jamdarkhana.'

I had to go carefully with that one. I had rehearsed it in my mind.

'It was my father's wish that everything should be left. Left where it was. That was what Dada-maharaj told me. Two days before he died. It is my wish too.'

It was like dropping a coin in a slot and waiting for the mechanism to act. The teak mask that was his face was incapable of registering emotions. He took some time to react. Then he said:

'Cannot any arrangements be made to remove everything to a place of safety? They say it was brought on the backs of thirty-two elephants.'

"Perhaps it could be done. But we...both Dada-maharaj and myself, decided it would be best this way. We have given up all rights to it. It should be left as it came to us.'

But he seemed to be well-versed in the rights and wrongs of this particular issue. 'This is not proper. It is not the Maharaja's own treasure... not yours or Dada-maharaja's. You may give up your right, but your son has a right too—and his son and his son; whoever happens to be the Bedar king.'

'My son and his son will never be rulers. I am the last one.' I explained. 'And thank God they will not be Maharajas,' I added.

Again the old man looked blankly at me for a few seconds, but there was still no sign of any understanding in his eyes. I might have been speaking a language he did not understand. Did those who were in charge of treasuse always have to be dumb?—I asked myself—their minds incapable of going off outside the grove of dog-like devotion to their jobs? I wondered if he took bhang or some other kind of dope.

'Let us be thankful that neither Dada-maharaj nor I were called upon to go in there for an emergency,' I said. 'He went only twice, and so am I, going only twice. . . .'

He shook his head. 'Dada-maharaj went in only once,' he said. 'Only once, when he was the Yuwaraj. He never came after he became the Maharaja. We requested him to come every year when he used to camp at Bulwara. He always made an excuse.'

'I want to go in now,' I told him.

At last his eyes lit up. 'I hope the Bedar king is going to treat this visit as an emergency.' he said softly.

I laughed, as much with relief at the measure of his response as with my own thoughts. 'A sort of emergency,' I said. 'Yes, something like that.'

'I shall go and make the arrangements, the lamps and everything.' He turned to go.

I stopped him. I had waited for him to ask me what was going to happen to his clan, almost shut away from the outside world for nearly two hundred years. But since he did not appear to think of it, I told him what I had in mind.

'I shall make provision for all of you. Put some of the older ones on pensions and try to give the others some land. You need not be afraid of the future.'

He gave me a level stare. 'We have never worried about that, Bedar King,' he said. 'We knew that the Bedar would not forsake us. There is an oath that binds us to him. We never had any fear that the Bedar king would leave us in the wind.'

It was a pathetic kind of loyalty. I had half a mind to tell the old man to go and help himself to some of the gold, but I knew it would have shocked him to the core.

I did not stay in the room with the oil-flame lamps for long. I had not even curiosity left. I had taken with me the two duelling pistols, oiled and cleaned and looking almost ready for use. I put them back in the faded velvet case which had been their resting place since the days of Louis XIII. They fitted snugly, butt to muzzle, back into the dents they had made for themselves. Even during the minute or so I was there, I was beginning to be conscious of the smell of dead roses emanating from the garments in the boxes. Moved by some impulse I cannot explain, I sat down briefly on the golden throne of prince Murad. And then I got up and walked out, aware of a good deed done, of a debt paid off, that whatever my father and I had removed from the place of curses had been given back.

I had made up my mind to leave Begwad for a few months as soon as the inauguration of the new administration was over. I was mentally braced for what was coming. Indeed, I had a feeling that all things considered, I had performed my tasks without discredit. But I wanted my wife and children to be away from Begwad at the time of the inauguration ceremonies. I wanted to be alone on my last day as the ruler of Begwad, and I was a little annoyed when I found that my wife was reluctant to go away.

'I want to be here,' Kamala told me with unaccustomed firmness. 'I am the Maharani; I too want to see it through.'

'It is all over already,' I said. 'There is nothing more to see through. It is... it is like waiting for the train to pull out after the good-byes have been said.'

'We will just send the children away with Miss Groves', she said. 'I want to remain here. I am your wife. It is my duty to remain by your side. It is also my right.'

'I want to be alone for this, Kamala,' I said, 'and don't say 'I want to be here' again.'

'It feels so horrible... quite shameful. Like running away. Leaving you alone to face things, in your adversity.'

Her voice broke down. She was leaning forward, with her teeth pressing her lower lip, her eyes bright with moisture, and the way the light fell on her face, she looked breath-takingly lovely. I caught her face in my hands and kissed her gently on the nose, and then I gathered her into my arms and held her close to me.

I went on holding her, concious of a sudden lifting away of tension, pressing my face into the softness of her chest and grateful for its comfort and warmth.

'The door is open and the butler will be bringing in tea at any minute,' Kamala reminded me.

I did not release her. 'You must train the servants not to bring tea at inconvenient moments.' I mumbled.

She ran her fingers through my hair. 'There haven't been many inconvenient moments lately,' she pointed out.

I released her then. 'Why do you want to be here?' I asked.

'Because I want to be near you. Besides....'

'Besides what'?

'It's just that I don't want you to face it alone. You might do something a little rash, something which someone close to you, someone who loves you, might be able to prevent.'

'Do you think I am going to break down'?

'I know you won't.'

'Then what'?

'Darling, don't be angry, but I feel so frightened.'

'Frightened'! I felt like laughing. 'What is there to be frightened of, now? They cannot take away any more than they have.'

No, they could do no more damage. It had come and gone, like a tremor in the earth; now there was only the debris. The debris and those who were near and dear to you, those who wanted to stand by you.

'Please don't be bitter. They can take away much more. We still have so much.'

'I am not being bitter,' I protested, 'I am completely relaxed.'

'Relaxed!' Kamala shook her head. 'No, you are not relaxed. You are tense, knotted up. You mumble in your sleep and gnash your teeth and say things. I have lain awake for hours, terrified, not knowing whether to wake you.'

'You should have. What have I been mumbling?'

'It is all rather indistinct. Sometimes it is like some verse. Something like 'the vengeance of sheep can be a terrible thing.' But most of the time you keep repeating "This I have sworn, this I swear".'

'Oh.'

'Abhay, what is it that you have sworn? What are you going to do? Sometimes you act so much like your father that it makes me feel frightened. Darling, you are not alone. There are your children, there is me. We are not outsiders...'

'I can't think what I could have been dreaming about,' I told her. 'But please listen to me. I want you to go. Not because you are an outsider, but just because you are so near to me. I want you to go away for my own sake, because I love you.'

The words had slipped out of my mouth as though at a confessional and Kamala stared at me for a few seconds. Then I saw her wipe her eyes with the end of her sari. 'You have never told me that before,' she said. 'I have always hoped that you would, some day.'

'Always is so long.' I said. 'Always is ever so long.'

Kamala looked at me anxiously. 'Darling, what are you talking about?'

I laughed. 'Sometimes it comes after many years... it cannot be there in the madness of youth... and then one day it hits you...'

'What are you saying?' Kamala said again.

'I am telling you that I love you,' I told her, and I felt wholly sincere as I said it.

'It is nice to be loved. It seems silly to talk of love after two children... but it feels, it feels wonderful. Please give me your handkerchief.'

I gave her my handkerchief. 'Once this is over, we will go on a honeymoon,' I said. 'We'll go to strange, exotic places, romantic places.'

'What is it that you are afraid of, Abhay?' she asked. 'What do you think is going to happen'?

Somehow I did not resent her curiosity. Suddenly I wanted to tell her, share my burden with her.

'I really don't know.' I said. 'It is just a vague feeling. Something to do with the Bhils. I don't think they quite trust me. And if they start an agitation or anything like that, they will come in for a lot of punishment. They are our charge, the Bhils. I don't want them to be hurt more than can be helped.'

'But you have done your best. You can have nothing to blame yourself about.'

'It is so difficult to see one's way clearly through all this. For one thing, they will be finished as a separate clan, as a distinct ethnological sub-heading: the Bhils of Bulwara. They are all grouped together now, because they live in the valley. It will not be possible for the Government to resettle them all together. . . .'

We went on talking, as man and wife, about our problems. I was grateful to find someone I could confide in, to whom I could pour out the doubts that had been haunting me.

In the end, I was able to persuade her to go away with the children. Three days before the durbar, I drove my family to the station. There was a lump in my throat as the train moved away, carrying my son and my daughter waving wildly, and my wife poised, smiling and dignified and tearless—a Maharani conscious of the need for keeping up appearances.

As I stood looking at the departing train, I had a feeling that the play was coming to an end, and I was aware of the dramatic neatness of the ending. I was eager for the last three days to pass, for the end to be clean and swift.

It was the day before the final durbar. I was sitting on the balcony of my father's bedroom, sorting out the papers in his desk which I had arranged in neat piles on the glass-topped coffee table before me, when I heard the crunching of car wheels on the gravel drive leading to the main porch. Very few cars were permitted to use the main gate or the central porch of the palace, and I remember thinking that one of the other rulers who had come for the durbar had come to pay me a call.

A few minutes later I heard the sound of footsteps on the carpet behind me. I was reading one of my own letters, sent to my father from college, describing a cricket match and explaining why I had not done better in the Sanskrit paper, I was still a part of that moment, more than ten years in the past. I looked round in annoyance and stared at the woman who stood in the doorway wearing a white sari. It took me a second or two to realize that she was my mother. For a moment I wondered why she was wearing a widow's white and had come out without the red dot on her forehead which was compulsory for all Hindu wives, and then my mind was back in the present.

It was more than six years since I had seen my mother, but I was not surprised that she looked as strikingly lovely as ever. Middle age had only added a sort of chiselled perfection to her features.

Whose fault was it that we had not seen each other for all those years? Hers or mine? Or was it no fault of either of us?

She came and sat down on the wicker chair on the other side

of the coffee table, and looked at me with a touch of anxiety, just as she had whenever I came home from school or college.

'Don't say 'How thin you have become!' Maji,' I said.

She gave me a quick smile. There were wrinkles round her eyes that had not been there before. 'But you are looking thin, Abhay. You look as though you haven't been sleeping well.'

'You are looking just as you always did,' I told her.

Mother smiled again. 'Tell me, Abhay, is this thing getting you down too much'?

'I expect it is, rather. But it is all going to be over tomorrow. And I sleep very well, Mother, like a log.'

'You must get away from all this. Go away for a long time.'

'I am going, Maji. We are all going to Calcutta. Then I want to go to Mussorie. Perhaps a trip to Europe later in the year.'

It was extraordinary how we had slipped into a groove of conversation as though we had been seeing each other every day. Or was there something brittle, something artificial in the things we had been saying, as though we were subconsciously trying to cover up our real feelings behind the banalities of small talk?

'I have missed you, Abhay. You are the only person connected with all this... with my past, that I have really missed,' Mother said. 'That I will go on missing.'

Her words made a small smear of guilt on my conscience, for on my part I had not missed her at all. 'I hope you have come to live here, Maji,' I said. I had a feeling that the ice was breaking up, that we were no longer being protected by the screen of small talk.

She shook her head slowly, taking a long time to answer.

Then she said, 'No, Abhay, quite the opposite, in fact. I have come to say good-bye.'

'Where are you going, Maji'?

'I am going to Karachi; to Pakistan.'

'With that... with Abdula Jan'?

She winced, her face paled, her eyes hardened. 'As you wanted to say, with *that* man.'

'But you cannot go there, Maji. It is foreign territory now. They are killing thousands of Hindus every day. It is here that you belong. With us.'

'No I don't belong here. I belong there, on the other side of the border.'

Something in her expression made me ask:

'Have you... you haven't married him, have you'?

She looked straight into my eyes, almost defiantly. 'We were married last week.'

'You are nothing but a bitch, a shameless woman of the streets! You cheap whore!' I cried out, stung by I know not what tortured emotions. And I realised the horror of my words only when I saw the shock and the anger in her face. I hung my head in shame and disgust. 'I am sorry Mother,' I said. That was all there was to say.

'I may be a bitch, but I am no longer a shameless woman of the streets. I was one, all these years when I lived with a man in sin. But remember I had been abandoned by my husband—I was a discarded woman.' Her eyes were hard, her voice dry, her words like the pricks of a scalpel.

'I am sorry, Maji,' I said again. 'Please forgive me.' My own private life was a morass of guilt. Who was I to talk of sin, of abstract standards of morals? I who had never been faithful to Kamala and carried no taint of sin within me, what right had I to feel outraged at my mother's degradation?

But my mother did not want to forgive me easily. It was her right to punish me for the pain I had caused her. Her face, which had no make-up, was dead white, and had the hardness of glass.

'A bitch but not a whore any more... now that I am married.'

'I'm sorry, Mother.'

'And yet it was you who gave me the courage to run away from misery to happiness...to a man I loved. It was then that I felt that you were at least partly mine—not wholly his.'

'I hope you are happy, Maji. I hope you have found what you were seeking.'

'Who can say what anyone is seeking? And yet I can say I am happy—happy because I have found what I never had, a place of honour in a man's house. I am the wife, the lady of the house, share in the joys and sorrows of the husband. Here I was nothing. I was never even told when they operated on your nose—as though I had nothing to do with you.'

'It was I who wanted no one to be told, Maji,' I said. 'I wanted to spare you the anxiety.'

'And do you know this is the first time that I have entered this room, his room, when all those other women, one after the other, even my maid-servants were admitted. They came and sat here, sat where you are sitting... shared his bed. I never came. I was only the wife, the Maharani, confined to the end of the palace.'

'Please, Mother,' I implored. 'Please.' She was hurting me and I knew she would go on hurting me, but I deserved it all.

'I am no longer something to be hidden like sin, hidden behind bamboo curtains as though I had some kind of deformity. It was—it was like being an animal, a leper kept in segregation, until I went away, preferring to be a woman of the streets, as you have said, to being a Maharani in darkness...never knowing what it was to be a complete woman.'

'Have you changed your religion too'? I asked. "Become a Muslim'?

'Yes.'

'Oh, my God!' I said. 'Oh, my God!'

'Why don't you say it? Why don't you say what is in your mind'? she taunted me.

'I have nothing to say, Mother. Nothing.'

I had nothing to say. All I could think of was her ardent, almost passionate devotion to her gods, her veneration for the seven satis in the family, of the time when I entered her prayer room and she had tears in her eyes. And then I found myself thinking of my father's religion, flamboyant, loud, almost defiant. I was glad he was not alive to be subjected to this final mortification—the Bedar Maharani marrying her lover and changing her religion.

'And I can assure you that I did not become a Mohammedan because he wanted me to, but because I wanted to belong to my husband's religion, belong completely to him.... hold nothing back that I had to give.'

There was a soft buzzing in my head, and somewhere at the back a nerve pounded as though it were going to burst. Why was I being given this extra punishment? Was this my reward for venerating the father-image I had created in my mind out of a man who was a good rifle shot and who made a fetish of manliness, teaching me never to break down under punishment, never to squeal, the man who quoted from the scriptures to justify his waywardness in thought or in action? This was his retribution, not mine—the punishment was rightly his.

'I came because I wanted to see you before I went away. But perhaps it was inevitable that you should cause me this additional pain, just at the moment of parting. When an illusion that one had nursed all one's life is shattered it cannot help hurting. To think that for all those years, it was you that kept me here, for whose sake I was willing to go on enduring, whom I went on loving even when you disowned me the moment I did what I should have done... you, the embodiment of purity abandoning something which had been polluted, you who could bring yourself to call your mother a whore'!

'It wasn't me, Mother, you know it wasn't,' I cried out, 'It was something that possessed me... it was...'

She gave a hard, bitter laugh. 'You asked whether I had found what I was seeking. What I was seeking was just what you accused me of— what a woman's body and mind burn for.'

'Oh, please, please, Mother.'

'It was you who mattered. You who caused me the pain when you disowned me... when you stopped writing and I used to lie awake for news of you, haunted by forebodings. You who kept me tied to this place; not him. And when he died, I'm not ashamed to say that I could not even bring myself to feel sorry—I who cannot prevent myself from crying when one of my canaries gets hurt. That is what you and he have done to me.'

'He is dead now, Mother,' I said in sudden exasperation. 'Do you mind not saying anything about him'?

She stared at me in anger, almost as though I had said something rude. 'Oh I should have known better,' she said. 'You were always his boy; his in spite of everything I did for you. I am sorry I was carried away. You will always be what you are, and I will always love you, my son, my only son.'

I said nothing, I hung my head.

'I think I had better go now' my mother said, and her voice was normal again. 'There is no point in lingering here. Good-bye, and God bless you'!

No, there was no point in her lingering in the room, my father's room which had been denied to her all the time she had lived in the palace. I found myself wishing she would go.

She stood up and walked away, as she had always walked, with the grace of a court dancer leaving the stage after bowing to the applause, walked away as though unaware that she was taking with her a part of myself.

In the archway, she stopped. 'I almost forgot,' she said. 'I have settled my affairs, here... the house and the land and things. They are yours, I want you to take them. The papers are with Harikishore. . . .'

'I have no use for your estates, Maji,' I said. 'I have enough of my own.'

'Who knows, some day you might have need of them, the way things seem to be going with you.'

'And how will you live, Mother'?

'I will live as a wife should live, on what her husband gives her,' she said proudly, almost defiantly, and then she added: 'I am going as I came, taking nothing from here; a woman, not a Maharani.'

And then she was gone.

I wanted to shout to her to stop, to get up and run after her, try and comfort her and comfort myself, assuage the wounds of my mind as I had done in the past. But I did nothing of the kind. I sat gazing at the spot where she had stood, under the marble arch with the lotus design, knowing that I should never see my mother again.

(From *The Princes*, The Viking Press, New York, 1963)

The Fixer

LALA Govind Sarup, addressed by everyone as 'Lalaji' and referred to as 'The Fixer,' peered at the mud-coloured cyclostyled sheet with fierce concentration. It was the Minister's tour programme.

The Fixer, who had trained himself to read between the lines even of official tour programmes, pushed back his glasses and smiled to himself. The fact that he had been sent a copy of the tour programme at all, meant that the Minister wished to see him. The entry for Raniwada, where the Minister was camping for two days, was underlined in red ink. So it was in Raniwada that the Minister wished to see him. It was as good as an invitation. It would mean an eighty-mile bus journey, but of course, you couldn't think of disregarding a Minister's invitation.

The Fixer called for his silver pan-dan and busied himself with the ceremony of making his first pan of the day. He was still chewing the same pan a half-hour later when Arjun Dass, Chandumal Marwari's son, came to see him. He lay back in

The Fixer

his chair, his eyes half-closed, while Arjun Dass rambled on about his family, about how narrowly he had missed getting a university degree, and similar qualifications.

'So, father thinks I should get a job; a steady, Government job,' Arjun Dass concluded.

'Yes, I see that,' the Fixer mumbled. 'In your walk of life... no other kind of job would be suitable... but you know how difficult things are getting every day.'

'You, Lalaji, can create a job where no job exists,' Arjun Dass said with his most ingratiating smile. 'Everybody knows that.'

But the Fixer refused to be flattered, 'Tell your father I'll see what I can do.' He told his visitor. 'Jobs—Government jobs—are not easy, these days. It will mean a visit to the Secretariat... possibly see the Minister himself. Very difficult!'

So, that was what Chandumal's son was after; a Government job. It was a big price Chandumal was asking. On the other hand Chandumal had done something equally big for the Fixer; his niece's marrying into the Zamindar's family would not have been possible if Chandumal hadn't helped. Unfortunately, the horoscopes had been conflicting, and Chandumal had brought pressure on the Pandits to certify that they were matching.

Late in the afternoon, Tukaram Dhore came to see him. Tukaram belonged to a nearby Harijan village. 'Lalaji, please read this letter for me,' he said, placing a yellow typed sheet on the table.

The Fixer took a long time to read the few lines, frowning deeply all the while. He had to play this carefully, thinking two moves ahead. Tukaram waited nervously, wiggling his toes.

'It is a letter from the Commissioner Saheb. It says that yo have won the first prize in the district for the highest yield of rice,' the Fixer told him.

'Jai Ambadevi!' Tukaram exclaimed, 'What will I get, money? —a gold medal?'

The Fixer shook his head sadly, 'Most likely you will get a paper certificate—and a whole lot of trouble to go with it.'

'Trouble, Lalaji!'

'Yes, you will have to visit the capital, two days away by train, and talk to the big people there, even see the Minister himself. As you know, it takes weeks to see a Minister. You will have to give a speech on the radio, and all the Kheti sahibs will ask you questions; what methods did you use?—What manures?—What...'

'But, Lalaji, I used no methods, it was just a good year, when the rain-god and the manure-god and the wind-god and the god who protects cattle and crops were on the side of the farmer, and Ambadevi has blessed me. And how can I go to the big city, tell me, leaving my wife with the new-born baby? And the radio! —arrere! Lalaji, please tell me what I can do to be spared this trouble—you who solve everybody's troubles!'

'It is all very difficult, very very difficult,' the Fixer said with half-closed eyes 'Still, something has to be done, must be done,' and for a long time he lay back in his chair, rubbing his shaven head with the palm of his hand. Then he said:

'I think you'd better tell everyone that your high yield was entirely due to Arjun Dass's improved agricultural methods...'

'What! Who! Lalaji? Chandumal's son?'

'Well, you just say that Arjun Dass told you what to do: about manuring, and weeding and transplanting. If someone asks you any questions, just tell them to go and ask Chandumal's son...'

'But, Lalaji, Arjun Dass has not spoken to me since the elephant-god festival. How can... and how much will he charge me for all this?' he asked, suddenly suspicious.

The Fixer waved his hands magnanimously. 'No, no. No-no-no-no-no, he won't charge you anything. I'll see to that. Now you just go and tell Chandumal Marwari and his son what I said. And I will do my best to keep you out of trouble. Of course, it will mean a lot of extra expense to me—and trouble. I'll have

The Fixer

to see the officials, perhaps the Minister himself...'

'Lalaji, you are as kind as Rama himself; may Ambadevi bless you,' Tukaram said with folded hands.

When a few days later, the Fixer went to Raniwada to see the Minister, he was wondering what the Minister wanted to see him about. So, he was quite taken aback when the Minister asked him instead: 'What can I do for you?'

It took the Fixer only a few seconds to adjust himself to this new approach, while the Minister waited, leaning forward in his chair, eager, smiling-faced.

'Everyone talks about food shortage, but people are saying that no one does anything about growing more food,' the Fixer said.

'We are doing everything we can, to teach modern methods, modern farming methods, to our farmer bhais,' the Minister began to quote from his own speech given at a reception recently. 'Show our kisan brothers by giving demonstrations, how it is done in advanced countries. Foreign methods have been found...'

'Chi, chi, chi, chi,' said the Fixer, making a face. 'Foreign methods! That is what our farmer bhais don't like. Foreign means anti-national! Chi, Chi.'

'Then our farmer bhais must be made to realise...' the Minister began.

'What we say is, why not encourage our own methods? Our scientists, our research pioneers?' the Fixer cut in. 'This Arjun Dass in our town has worked miracles in our villages. Wonders! No extra expense, no machinery, nothing like foreign methods— chi, chi! He has doubled the crop in our villages and nearly tripled it in one farm.'

'Really!' said the Minister blinking his eyes.

'Wonders! And all due to Arjun Dass's guidance; his improved agricultural methods. It would be, er, of enormous value if,— practical farmers were to be given due recognition... our own men should come before foreign experts. Now, if he were to be appointed to some Government post without delay... an agricultural adviser to the district, or something like that. That would prove to the people that the Government is always ready to put first things first...'

'But there is no post for an agricultural adviser to your district, or any other district,' the Minister said uncertainly.

The Fixer smiled his most meaningful smile. 'If your honour wishes, your honour can always create a post, an experimental post. In the national interest, for the sake of our own kisan brothers. Temporary at first, of course...'

'Well,' the Minister said, 'Hmmmm, perhaps something could be done. What did you say the man's name was? Arjun Singh? And mind you, it can only be a temporary appointment...'

'All Government jobs are temporary—at first,' said the Fixer, and he and the Minister laughed as though at a shared joke.

At the same time, the Fixer was aware that he hadn't been promised anything. So far everything had gone smoothly, perhaps too smoothly, but the real catch was yet to come.

At last, the Minister came out with it: 'I'm greatly worried about the Harijan votes,' he said. 'They didn't amount to much in my last constituency, but in this one, where I have been given my ticket now, you know there is a big Harijan population and...'

'The way things are going, a high-caste Brahmin will always have to worry about the votes of those of our bhais who are considered untouchable by some,' the Fixer philosophised, trying to play it safe.

'It is very sad,' the Minister said, shaking his head in sadness. 'They don't know who are their real benefactors; those of us who hold nothing more sacred than the cause of our Harijan bhais.'

'I will get a purely Harijan village to give you an address of welcome,' the Fixer announced triumphantly, 'acclaiming you as the champion of the Harijan cause. You get your radio and cinema and newspapers to give you full publicity...'

'Really!' the Minister exclaimed sitting up in his chair. 'Really! You are not trying to...I mean...'

'You just leave it to me. You just get your photographers and others to be there...'

'But perhaps you don't know... not aware that since the last election I have had to, most reluctantly of course, decline every single invitation from the Harijan communities. You know how these things happen. I mean... it will be a very difficult matter to get our Harijan brothers to give me an address of welcome. In fact, I must confess I don't remember to have spoken to a single Harijan for years.' the Minister blurted out.

'You leave that to me, sir,' said the Fixer. 'You just arrange for the photographers and the radio people. And by the way, the name of the man is Arjun Dass, not Arjun Singh here let me write it down for you.'

While in town, the Fixer who was nothing if not thorough also remembered to buy a copy of The Farmer's Guide from the Government book depot, and when, upon his return, Arjun Dass came to see him, he brought out the book.

'Tell your father your job is fixed,' he told Arjun Dass. 'Agricultural Assistant to the District Commissioner.'

'Agricultural what? Arerere! I have never done a day's farming in my life... I mean... really I cannot tell the difference between a wheat crop and a rice crop.'

'I have thought of all that,' said the Fixer. 'Here, take this. You'd better study it closely,' and he gave Arjun Dass the copy of the Farmer's Guide.

'You think this will teach me about farming methods.'

'Improved farming methods,' corrected Lala Govind Sarup. 'By the time they find out you don't know anything about farming, you will have learnt enough for them to make you permanent.'

Tukaram Dhore saw Lalaji's tonga come to a halt in front of

his door, and came out with folded hands. 'What happened in the city?' he asked.

'Don't ask me,' said the Fixer, looking glum. 'Don't ask me. Oh, the things you people make me do! But you too are a lucky man. That's why I could do something. Very lucky, you are. It was very difficult, but I have solved everything.'

'I knew you would, Lalaji, May mother Amba bless you.'

'It took all my influence, but in the end I have arranged that you shouldn't have to go all the way to the Capital to receive your prize.'

'No!'

'No, instead, I have arranged that the Minister himself should come here; here, to your village, do you realise, so that you should be saved the trouble.'

'Is this true? Arre, Ram Ram! The Minister Sahib, himself!'

'The Honourable Minister Sahib himself!'

'Coming to this village?'

'Coming to this village. Leaving al his work, and coming here, only to give you your prize. So will you gather all your Harijan bhais so that they witness this great event of your Minister coming all the way here just to give you your prize? All the bhais from all the nearby villages.'

'That I will, Lalaji.'

'And give the Minister a welcome such as no one has been given in this village' I shall write a speech, a very short speech which you can learn by heart, and the schoolboys will sing songs, and shower flowers, and the women will do pooja with lighted lamps. And everyone will cheer...'

'Yes, yes, yes, yes,' said Tukaram, completely carried away, 'I will see that every Harijan from the twenty-four villages comes to cheer the Minister Sahib. Lalaji, but how can I repay you for bringing this great honour to this village, and to our community. The bag of rice I give you every year for reading and writing my letters and applications will hardly compensate for one hundredth of what you have done for me...'

'Nonsense, man, nonsense!' exclaimed the Fixer, beating a hasty retreat. 'Here, no, no, you mustn't touch my feet! Chi, oh, no-no-no-no,' and he jumped into his tonga with a horrified look on his face, hoping that no passer-by had witnessed his feet being touched by Tukaram. For Lala Govind Sarup, too, was a Brahmin of the highest class.

(From *A Toast in Warm Wine*, Hind Poeket Books, 1974, New Delhi, 1974.)

5. KAMALA MARKANDAYA

Kamala Markandaya is a South Indian by birth, parentage, and education and has worked as a journalist both in India and England. She usually, but not invariably, uses India as the setting for her novels, and made her debut on the British literary scene with *Nectar in a Sieve* in 1954. She lives in London, is married and has a daughter.*

Nectar in a Sieve, reminiscent of Thomas Hardy's novels, paved the way for a succession of fine books: *Some Inner Fury* (1955), *A Silence of Desire* (1960), *Possession* (1963), *A Handful of Rice* (1966), *The Coffer Dams* (1969), *The Nowhere Man* (1972), *Two Virgins* (1973) and *The Golden Honeycomb* (1977). These novels reveal her careful craftsmanship and her precise use of the English language. But Markandaya's forte is in recording and describing the inner workings of a character's mind and heart; as well as in 'the delicate analysis of the relation of persons...particularly when they are attempting to grope towards some more independent existence' (William Walsh). Her anti-colonialist and anti-imperialist stance comes through in her works, but there is little or no hysteria in her writing, and her social pronouncements are always tempered with common sense and sound judgement. *The Nowhere Man* is a case in point.

The Nowhere Man, as the title suggests, is a study in alienation; it is also a study in race-relations and a chronicle of Srinivas's fifty years in England. Arriving in London with his wife Vasantha, Srinivas opens a small spice-shop. Here, two sons, Laxman and Seshu, are born to them, and they buy an old house in south London so that they can all live together. But tragedy moves in swiftly. Seshu is killed by a German flying bomb during the war and Vasantha dies of tuberculosis. Srinivas is left alone— his son Laxman having rejected him after marrying an English girl from a comfortably well-off family in Plymouth. Ambling along the street one day, he meets Mrs Pickering—a divorcee somewhat older than himself to whom he becomes attached. Having no one to care for her, she moves in with Srinivas and brings some warmth into his life. Short of funds, they take in tenants, only to turn them out later when it is found Srinivas has leprosy and must be quarantined in his house. Opposition against him is organised by Fred Fletcher, the good-for-nothing son of a kindly woman who has compassion for Srinivas. Fred Fletcher beats up Srinivas, tars and feathers him, starts false rumours, and places faeces on his doorsteps to harass him. But the gentle and soft-spoken Srinivas accepts his lot stoically and finally dies when his house is set on fire. Says a neighbour, Mrs Glass, to Mrs Pickering :

'You mustn't blame yourself,' said Mrs Glass, sweating.

'Blame myself,' said Mrs Pickering. 'Why should I ? I cared for him.'

'And, indeed, that seemed to her to be the core of it,' says the author in what is also the last line of the book. Like E.M. Forster, Kamala Markandaya puts personal relationship above everything else and sees in such relationship the hope of a better future. In this complex novel she may well be saying that the 'nowhere man' is not really Srinivas who is capable of both loving and engendering love. The 'nowhere man' is perhaps Laxman, who, as he rejects his father, is himself rejected by the land of his birth. The 'nowhere man' could also be Fred Fletcher in whose life there is no room for love and understanding. It is they who are lost.

*Kamala Markandaya is reluctant to talk about her life and background, preferring her work to speak for itself.

What follows is Chapter 26 of the novel. Mrs Pickering has helped Mrs Fletcher to prepare her dead husband for burial and as such has earned the privilege to ride behind the cortege to the cemetery. Accompanying Mrs Pickering is Srinivas, who informs her serenely of the disease that is consuming him.

The Nowhere Man

Mr Fletcher was buried, wrapped in a shroud, encased in a coffin, embedded in the earth.

His widow went to his funeral riding in a shiny black Bentley. In another rode Mrs Pickering, with Srinivas beside her, wearing gloves on his hands. For Mrs Fletcher had insisted.

'After all you did,' she said, her pale eyes flickering, looking anywhere but at the woman she addressed, while invisible words scrambled around saying: after what *Fred* has done, so hectically that it brought the blood to her cheeks.

'I did very little,' said Mrs Pickering, with truth, but unable to deny the gesture, whatever it was, that this wan, courageous woman was making.

'I am a sick man,' said Srinivas, also with truth, though the full extent of it he could not reveal.

'A short service, it will not take long,' said Mrs Fletcher, limp but stubborn, and lied on an inspired note. 'Mr Fletcher would have wished it.'

Mr Fletcher's wishes, of course, had not been ascertainable for some considerable time and now never would be, but Fred Fletcher made his own view plain.

'If that bloody wog goes anywhere near my father's grave there'll be trouble,' he declared, banging the table and breaching the reverent membrane that hung, as frail as a caul at imminent birth, in this hushed house of the dead.

Mrs Fletcher did not deign to reply. She gazed at the drawn blinds and her lips tightened, but she suffered in silence. After the funeral, she promised herself, and made nebulous, daring resolutions that rocked her even as she sat.

Srinivas also postponed. He set up the interment in front of him like a deadline, before which there were certain things to do, and after which there would be certain actions to take. For the three-day respite thus gained he made up a meticulous timetable, plotting each hour and filling it so that it could lead to the next, and the next, and so reach, without undue severity, redemption date of the bond he had sealed with himself.

The third day went by. The date was advanced to the fourth and the fifth, then indefinitely. Keyed up to deeds, his hours carefully charted, Srinivas felt there was nothing with which to continue. He grew hollow, from want of substance with which to mold existence, while the inner surfaces of his body and mind were stretched and glazed with the tension of the situation, and what had been respite took on the aspects of nightmare.

Meanwhile Mr Fletcher also waited, all stiff and unknowing, on a trestle table rigged up in the crowded funeral parlor. They had embalmed him once, just enough to render him innocuous yet presentable; now they carried him to inner rooms and gutted him thoroughly, in the interests of hygiene in general and their own health in particular.

'Can't be too careful,' said the funeral director to his assistants 'in this business. See what's happening?' He twitched at the sheet and uncovered Mr Fletcher's hapless middle, around which a furry girdle was sprouting. 'That's putrefaction. Damn and blast their bloody guts.' He meant the gravediggers, whose strike had brought the corpse to this plight, though the newer of his assistants, concluding falsely, thought the wording unseemly, but soon had his faith revived by his director's manner on the telephone.

'Oh, no madam,' he was saying, as he had already said to several distracted bereaved, in tones which blended concern nicely with reassurance, in a voice pitched—but not so low as to render him incomprehensible—at that reverent level proper to this transit camp of the departed. 'Oh, no, there is no difficulty, our premises are more than adequate, and if I may say so, madam, you would find everything most tastefully arranged... that is, if you would care to visit?'

Most would not, he knew; they ran from death, but dead bodies really had them bolting down the aisles. He banked on it, though for safety's sake he did set aside one smallish room, in which three coffined corpses were on show, capable of rapid substitution and disposed like wares in a Bond Street window, which effectively demolished any suspicion of congested counters within. Nicely done, he thought to himself; very nicely done indeed. Not for nothing were his premises crowded.

So Mrs Fletcher composed herself to wait, with a certain bleak cheer that, unlike some, she had at least got her husband as far as the undertaker's.

In the fifteen days before the gravediggers took up their spades again Srinivas's resolve wore thin. He did not know. He imagined it to be as sturdy as when he had conceived it. He drew gloves over his disfigured hands, and sat beside Mrs Pickering in the third black Bentley, the first two being full of Fletcher family. Discreetly, shapes behind curtains, the neighbors watched. Odd, was the consensus of opinion. Not even her own family, Mrs Glass said darkly, let alone kith and kin; Mrs Fletcher could only be assumed to be not quite all there. This verdict her son thoroughly endorsed, adding several refinements of his own as he climbed, glowering, but impotent in the face of his mother's indomitable resolve, not to mention her possession of the roof over his head, into the car after his mother.

Srinivas was not aware. He sat remotely, and watched the familiar streets go by, and absently raised and smoothed the nap of the arm rest which was suede, once some animal's hide, now dove-gray and lush under the yellow gloved tips of his fingers. The blinds at the window were drawn. He could not remember a car having blinds except—. Except in India, he thought; long ago, in his youth, he had seen motorcars with flowered curtains fluttering at the windows in which Muslim ladies rode, ladies in purdah who were as total a mystery to him as those English memsahibs who festooned themselves in mosquito netting: throat, face, topi, all bundled into one large steamy globe. Yes, India. A far country, thought Srinivas, gently, to which he would not return. Gently, too, he felt the bottle in his pocket, filled with the white powder of tablets he had bought, and crushed, and carefully funneled in. But he had no feeling about it: the bottle, the tablets, were only agents, he could not transfer to them the weight of his resolve.

No feeling then, nor even at the graveside, or for Mrs Fletcher, who he knew had been relieved of a burden. Others, though, were moved by him, Fletcher mourners who had not been infected by

Fred's phobias felt sorry for the thin old man in his striking gloves and faded coat who looked, they said to each other in suitably subdued tones, so sad, worn out by the death of a neighbor and friend.

The looks, however, were false; the wear was not due to Mr Fletcher, whom Srinivas had scarcely known and would not miss, but was caused by the strain of unscheduled waiting. The long wait for a stranger's funeral, which had pared away not only his visible flesh but also the bones of his resolution, leaving a kind of wickerwork which his blindness imagined intact.

After the funeral, he had said to himself. It was after the funeral now. Up in the attic Srinivas waited for Mrs Pickering to return; she had gone to Mrs Fletcher's to partake of something—baked meats, he thought she had said, but could not be sure. He had been invited too, but had declined. Between the uncertainty of what baked meats were (he had his suspicions) and the certainty of Fred's animus, even the need to be close to Mrs Pickering ceased to be overriding. So, alone, he waited, and pale yellow sunshine flooded in and bred light on the polished surfaces on which it fell, of which there were not many, only the posts of the bed that were shiny from hands, the many hands that had touched and rested upon and wrestled with and finally lifted and shouldered the awkward structure across two continents, and the exposed oak beams of the sloping ceiling which had acquired the glossy patina of age. Eschewing passion (kindled, once, by the sleek dovetails of a structure he and his grandfather had raised, and deliberately killed after its desecration) yet both, house and bed, were dear to him. As such he had bequeathed them: the one to Mrs Pickering, by whom he knew it would continue to be cherished, the bed to his son Laxman, though here he entered an area of doubt.

Laxman, Srinivas shook his head, not over the shortcomings of his son, which it never occurred to him to include in any reckoning, but about the gulf that had opened. Inch by inch, territory had yielded: as years went by, yard after yard with increasing speed were gobbled up, until the chasm appeared. Canyons, up whose rocky sides neither could clamber. Created by mighty forces, one would have thought, would one not? Questioning himself, Srinivas smiled faintly. Trivia was what these forces were composed of. Made up of manners, accents, the food one ate, the clothes upon one's back (for not all Laxman's invisible strictures had gone unremarked), the pathetic grains piling up to become a force. What granules, then, had gone into the shaping of his momentous resolution? Srinivas smiled, genuinely, faintly, once again, as he gave himself the answer. The color of his skin, which had begotten the dangling man; and the configurations upon it which marked him out as diseased. These grains, so mighty, grew pathetic even as he named them.

So deep was his reverie that Srinivas did not hear Mrs Pickering come in, nor her footsteps upon the stairs, nor see her figure framed in the open doorway. She had to speak to rouse him.

'Oh, there you are,' she said, in some kind of relief.

'Yes.' His mouth was suddenly, terrifyingly dry, faced by the practicalities of the situation. Philosophy had vanished.

'I was worried.'

'Why?'

'You looked so strange.'

'No.'

Condemned to monosyllables, it seemed to him, when what he needed were strings on which to thread the meaning of his act. Because, somehow, one could not bring it out baldly. For one's own preservation it had to emerge comely, as Dr Radcliffe had done it, the announcement illuminated like the miniature of an old manuscript, even if comely was the last thing, in honesty, one could say about death.

'Perhaps I did,' he managed.

'Did what?'

'Look a little strange.'

'Yes. Funerals are apt to induce these feelings.'

At last he saw a way. 'It was my funeral,' he said, 'induced them. I have decided to end my life.'

She studied him. Alarm, which had made her catch her breath, was already, almost under control.

'What for?' she asked, and removed her hand from her breast, which had ceased to heave.

'It is time,' he replied.

'Who is to say?' she said. 'It is not for us.'

Her calm, the decency of her manner, leavened the horror of the situation. As suddenly as he had been terrorized, serenity returned to Srinivas. As, like a belssing, it had done in the surgery, dispossessing the doctor, composing his patient.

'It is time,' he said simply, 'when one is made to feel unwanted, and liable, as a leper, to be ostracized further, perhaps beyond the limit one can reasonably expect of oneself.'

He rose, and drew her to the window, from where they could view the dangling man—his outlines at any rate, since council workmen had been sent to wipe the slate clean as they were sent almost daily, an ineffectual routine reflected in a certain perfunctorniness of performance.

'You see,' he said.

'A few barren men,' she replied, and stood thickly, rebutting all that they represented, squalid policies to which the decent and incorruptible qualities of her constitution could clearly never be party. 'Is one to become a leper to oblige them?'

Then he did not know, became unsure as to whether it had been imagined to oblige; wavered and stared at his hands, which wore yellow gloves. Lemon-yellow. The shop had sold them, from old stock it had no ready sale for nowadays, and he had not objected. Though, as he now saw, they glared a bit: were, perhaps, too vivid for their purpose. As she, too, saw: had seen riding in the Bentley—indeed, had been unable to avoid—and had wondered, ascribing the donning of such gloves to some quirk, or a mistaken notion of appropriate apparel.

'To oblige, no,' he stammered. 'But, you see, it has happened.' And became calm, understanding that what was masked was real, whatever the chemistry of the change.

Under the gloves was disease. He took them off and showed her.

'The hospital has confirmed,' he said, 'Dr Radcliffe's suspicions, as well as my own knowledge which, I am ashamed to say, I have been fighting for some time.'

She remained standing. Lashed, it is true, by the same gales that had howled about his head, atavistic urges and old refrains that put bell and clapper on a man and sent him wandering. But standing. Her manner obdurate though wisps were flying, wild gray strands of hair escaped from coils and pins and pitching around in a frenzy. She tucked them back.

'It is curable,' she said.

'At my age?' he reminded. 'Are the means endurable, even if the end were not in some doubt?'

'Then what will you do?'

'I have told you.'

'That is the last,' she said flatly, 'of many solutions.' And she sat down to consider, the strength of her resolution forming like armor, some iron cladding of spiritual manufacture that would manifest to uphold her, right or wrong. Then he knew, in the middle of his own maelstrom understood better than he had ever done before why they made such good settlers: clung, where lesser mortals would have scuttled, and chipped and hammered away until whole landscapes altered, and original inhabitants turned into displaced persons.

'It is,' he ventured nevertheless, 'the only solution for me.' Wavering still, and conscious of drafts, and of holes enlarging in his decision, but aware all the while of a welding of their views.

'No,' she said again. 'That is not the solution.'

'What is?'

'Treatment,' she said, and would not meet his eyes. 'It is the only way.'

'I have already rejected it,' he said, with a bitterness born of disenchantment, having relied upon her strength but now, it seemed, to be driven back upon himself. As she had been. As all are in the end. A lesson which h at his age should have learned, only, Srinivas confessed to himself, there are these threadbare patches, these liquefying weaknesses of the soul.

'I have thought about it,' he amended 'but being old, it is not easy, since there are not many years left, and one would not wish to eke them out in prophylactic isolation.'

'Ah, no,' she said, rejecting, rejecting with all her might, which though formidable might yet prove powerless. 'No. They would not condemn you to that.'

'Their concern would be for the community, as it is right it should be,' he said, gently, because she was upset, being unused to defeats of this nature, or subjugation, as he had been. 'It would not be fair to override their interests for the sake of one individual.'

'The community,' she said—fought on, and would continue to fight, he saw, long after he had given up, 'need not be affected. You could be isolated here as well as in wards and cells, which are enough to drive anyone, as you have been driven. I would care for you, I am trained. There could be no objection, and the community will not be at risk.'

'They will think they are.'

'The doctors can correct their beliefs.'

'Nevertheless, they will believe what they want to believe, and there will be trouble.'

'In which case nothing need be revealed.' said Mrs Pickering, 'there is no onus on anyone to bring a hornets' nest about their ears.'

'But the others,' he cried in despair, 'they will be endangered. Or think they are. The house is full.'

Of encumbrances. As it should not have been, as his instincts had known, but he had overborne them. Barnacles, which one supposed salved the hulk, but in fact anchored the man whose destiny was to rise free.

'There are the tenants,' he said again, bleakly.

'They will have to be given notice,' said Mrs Pickering briskly.

'What can one tell them? They will want to know why.'

'Nothing,' she rejoined, 'as nothing can be told. We are not compelled to give reasons.' She mused for a while. 'I foresee little difficulty,' she said, 'as all the lodgings are furnished.'

(From *The Nowhere Man*, Allen Lane, 1963, London.)

6. R. K. NARAYAN

Among the most widely acclaimed novelists of our time, Rasipuram Krishnaswami Narayan was born in 1907 in Madras where he spent his early years. He was educated at Mysore where he settled down. His autobiography *My Days : A Memoir* (1976), gives a vivid account of his childhood, schooling, graduation and marriage. He started as a free-lance journalist and served for some time as co-editor of *Indian Thought*. Recognizing his *forte* to be fiction, he took to writing short stories and novels, which have come out at fairly regular intervals. His first work, *Swami and Friends* appeared in 1935— the year in which Mulk Raj Anand's first novel, *Untouchable* was also published. It was followed by *The Bachelor of Arts* (1937), *The English Teacher* (1945), *Mr Sampath* (1949), *Waiting for the Mahatma* (1955), *The Financial Expert* (1952), *The Guide* (1959), *The Man-Eater of Malgudi* 1961, *The Sweet Vender* (1967), and *The Painter of Signs* (1977). A collection of his stories, *An Astrologer's Day and Other Stories*, appeared in 1947. His reinterpretations of the Indian Classical lore appear in a volume entitled *The Ramayana*.

Though R.K. Narayan's themes are not extraordinary, they point to a vision of man that comes of a profound understanding of the human condition. An imaginary small town in Mysore state, Malgudi, provides the setting for several of his novels. But his milieu does not in any way make his works regional or narrow. He is at his best in depicting social comedy centred on a sensibility that is truly Indian. He employs 'a pure and limpid English' which is a consciously evolved medium, admirably suited to his purposes.

The Guide, R.K. Narayan's most popular novel, is primarily the story of Raju and his various roles as a guide. We first see him as a railway guide to tourists, then a kind of guide to a married woman called Rosie, and finally a guide to mankind. The last is a rather strange role which, unable to shake off, he reluctantly accepts.

Raju is a curious combination of disparate qualities: a romantic and a realist, a lover and a cheat, a clever manipulator and a drifter. He begins his life as railway Raju, gets involved with Rosie, wife of

Marco, who loves him. Rosie, neglected by her husband, is taken in by Raju's attention and desire to help her to become a dancer and thus realise her ambition. Raju is unequal to this task. As it turns out, he betrays her as well as himself by committing forgery for which he is imprisoned. On his release, he tries to begin life afresh and finds himself in a new role—that of a sadhu.

'Drift' seems to be the key-word that fits Raju's behaviour and growth. He drifts into various roles which he plays as well as he can. He makes no conscious attempt at becoming a 'guide.' However, once he is cast in a particular role, either by circumstances or by fate, he improvises like an actor; the story of his life is, indeed, one of improvisations. On his release from prison, Raju moves into the countryside in search of a new life. He takes refuge in an abandoned temple where he starts a school for village children. Here some of his vague and random utterances are mistaken for prophetic pronouncements by the simple village folk. They soon begin to revere him as a 'swami,' as a person endowed with spiritual powers. The most ardent of his devotees is Velan, who brings him food and takes care of all his needs.

Things, however, take a turn for the worse. A prolonged drought seems to threaten the countryside, and Raju's casual remark that he will not eat is misinterpreted by a young fellow to mean that the swami 'will not eat until it rains.' This spells disaster for Raju. He is offered no food, but adored by all as a saint who is fasting to bring about the much wanted rains. Moved by the people's faith in him, and faced with the grim reality of starvation, Raju decides to make a clean breast of his past to Velan. He tells Velan the whole story of his life to convince him that he is no 'swami' but an ordinary mortal subject to life's temptations and sins. But such indeed is Velan's faith in his master, that he accepts Raju's confessions as a part of Raju's greatness.

Entrapped by his own pronouncements and moved by the veneration of the people around him, Raju appears to live up to his assumed sainthood. On the last day of his fast, he goes down the steps of the river supported by Velan and another villager. Entering the water, he imagines that it is raining in the hills, and sags down. It is left to the reader's imagination to infer whether Raju dies or merely faints.

What follows is the last chapter of the novel:

The Guide

Raju's narration concluded with the crowing of the cock. Velan had listened without moving a muscle, supporting his back against the ancient stone railing along the steps. Raju felt his throat smarting with the continuous talk all night. The village had not yet wakened to life. Velan yielded himself to a big yawn, and remained silent. Raju had mentioned without a single omission every detail from his birth to his emergence from the gates of the prison. He imagined that Velan would rise with disgust and swear, 'And we took you for such a noble soul all along! If one like you does penance, it'll drive off even the little rain that we may hope for. Begone, you—before we feel tempted to throw you out. You have fooled us.' Raju waited for these words as if for words of reprieve. He looked on Velan's silence with anxiety and suspense, as if he waited on a judge's verdict again, a second time. The judge here seemed to be one of sterner cast than the one he had encountered in the court hall. Velan kept still—so still that Raju feared that he had fallen asleep.

Raju asked, 'Now you have heard me fully?' like a lawyer who has a misgiving that the judge has been wool-gathering.

'Yes, Swami.'

Raju was taken aback at still being addressed as 'Swami'. 'What do you think of it?'

Velan looked quite pained at having to answer such a question. 'I don't know why you tell me all this, Swami. It's very kind of you to address, at such length, your humble servant.'

Every respectful word that this man employed pierced Raju like a shaft. 'He will not leave me alone,' Raju thought with resignation. 'This man will finish me before I know where I am.'

After profound thought, the judge rose in his seat. 'I'll go back to the village to do my morning duties. I will come back later. And I'll never speak a word of what I have heard to anyone.'

He dramatically thumped his chest. 'It has gone down there, and there it will remain.' With this, he made a deep obeisance, went down the steps and across the sandy river.

A wandering newspaper correspondent who had come to the village picked up the news. The Government had sent a commission to inquire into the drought conditions and suggest remedies; and with it came a press correspondent. While wandering around he heard about the Swamiji, went to the temple across the river, and sent off a wire to his paper at Madras, which circulated in all the towns of India. 'Holy man's penance to end drought,' said the heading, and then a brief description followed.

This was the starting-point.

Public interest was roused. The newspaper office was besieged for more news. They ordered the reporter to go back. He sent a second telegram to say 'Fifth day of fast.' He described the scene. How the Swami came to the river's edge, faced its source, stood knee-deep in the water, from six to eight in the morning, muttering something between his lips, his eyes shut, his palms pressed together in a salute to the gods, presumably. It had been difficult enough to find knee-deep water—but the villagers had made an artificial basin in sand, and when it didn't fill, fetched water from distant wells and filled it, so that the man had always knee-deep water to stand in. The holy man stood there for two hours, then walked up the steps slowly, and lay down on a mat in the pillared hall of the temple, while his devotees kept fanning him continuously. He hardly took notice of anyone, though there was a big crowd around. He fasted totally. He lay down and shut his eyes in order that his penance might be successful. For that purpose he conserved all his energy. When he was not standing in the water, he was in deep meditation. The villagers had set aside all their normal avocations in order to be near this great soul all the time. When he slept they remained there, guarding him, and though there was a fair-sized crowd, it remained totally silent.

But each day the crowed increased. In a week there was a permanent hum pervading the place. Children shouted and played about, women came carrying baskets filled with pots, firewood, and foodstuffs, and cooked the food for their men and children. There were small curls of smoke going up all along the river bank, on the opposite slope, and on this bank also. It was studded with picnic groups, with the women's bright-coloured *sarees* shining in the sun; men too had festive dress. Bullocks unyoked from their carts jingled their bells as they ate the straw under the trees. People swarmed around little water-holes.

Raju saw them across his pillared hall whenever he opened his eyes. He knew what that smoke meant; he knew that they were eating and enjoying themselves. He wondered what they might be eating—rice boiled with a pinch of saffron, melted *ghee*—and what were the vegetables? Probably none in this drought. The sight tormented him.

This was actually the fourth day of his fast. Fortunately, on the first day he had concealed a little stale food, left over from the previous day, in an aluminium vessel behind a stone pillar in the innermost sanctum—some rice mixed with butter-milk and a piece of vegetable thrown in. Fortunately, too, he was able on the first day, to snatch a little privacy at the end of the day's prayer and penance, late at night. The crowd had not been so heavy then. Velan had business at home and had gone, leaving two others to attend on the Swami. The Swami had been lying on the mat in the pillared hall, with the two villagers looking on and waving a huge palmyra fan at his face. He had felt weakened by his day's fasting. He had suddenly told them, 'Sleep, if you like; I'll be back,' and he rose in a business-like manner and passed into his inner sanctum. 'I don't have to tell the fellows where I am going or why or how long I shall be gone out of sight.' He felt indignant. He had lost all privacy. People all the time watching and staring, lynx-eyed, as if he were a thief! In the inner sanctum, he briskly thrust his hand into a niche and pulled out his aluminium pot. He sat down behind the pedestal, swallowed his food in three or four large mouthfuls making as little noise as possible. It was stale rice, dry and stiff and two days old; it tasted awful, but it appeased his hunger. He washed it down with water. He went to the backyard and rinsed his mouth noiselessly—he didn't want to smell of food when he went back to his mat.

Lying on his mat, he brooded. He felt sick of the whole thing. When the assembly was at its thickest, could he not stand up on a high pedestal and cry, 'Get out, all of you, and leave me alone, I am not the man to save you. No power on earth can save you if you are doomed. Why do you bother me with all this fasting and austerity?' It would not help. They might enjoy it as a joke. He had his back to the wall—there was no further retreat. This realization helped him to get through the trial with a little more resignation on the second day of his penance. Once again he stood up in water, muttering with his face to the hills, and watching the picnic groups enjoying themselves all over the place. At night he left Velan for a while and sneaked in to look for leftover food in his aluminium vessel—it was really an act of desperation. He knew full well that he had polished the vessel the previous night. Still he hoped, childishly, for a miracle. 'When they want me to perform all sorts of miracles, why not make a start with my own aluminium vessel?' he reflected caustically. He felt weak. He was enraged at the emptiness of his larder. He wondered for a moment if he could make a last desperate appeal to Velan, to let him eat—and if only he minded, how he could save him! Velan ought to know, yet the fool would not stop thinking that he was a saviour. He banged down the aluminium vessel in irritation and went back to his mat. What if the vessel did get shattered? It was not going to be of any use. What was the point of pampering an empty vessel? When he was seated, Velan asked respectfully, 'What was that noise, master?'

'An empty vessel. Have you not heard the saying—an empty vessel makes much noise?'

Velan permitted himself a polite laugh, and declared with admiration, 'How many good sentiments and philosophies you have gathered in that head of yours, sir!'

Raju almost glared at him. This single man was responsible for his present plight. Why would he not go away and leave him alone? What a wise plan it would have been if the crocodile had got him while he crossed the river! But that poor old thing, which had remained almost a myth, had become dehydrated. When its belly was ripped open they found in it ten thousand rupees worth of jewellery. Did this mean that the crocodile had been in the habit of eating only women? No, a few snuff-boxes and ear-rings of men were also found. The question of the day was: Who was entitled to all this treasure? The villagers hushed up the affair. They did not want the Government to get scent of it and come round and claim it, as they did all buried treasure. They gave out that only a couple of worthless trinkets had been found inside the crocodile, although in actual fact the man who cut it open acquired a fortune. He had no problems for the rest of his life. Who permitted him to cut open the crocodile? Who could say? People didn't wait for permission under such circumstances. Thus had gone on the talk among the people about the crocodile when it was found dead.

Velan, fanning him, had fallen asleep—he had just doubled up in his seat with the fan in his hand. Raju, who lay awake, had let his mind roam and touch the depths of morbid and fantastic thought. He was now touched by the sight of this man hunched in his seat. The poor fellow was tremendously excited and straining himself in order to make this penance a success, providing the great man concerned with every comfort—except, of course, food. Why not give the poor devil a chance, Raju said to himself, instead of hankering after food which one could not get, anyway. He felt enraged at the persistence of food-thoughts. With a sort of vindictive resolution, he told himself, 'I'll chase away all thought of food. For the next ten days I shall eradicate all thoughts of tongue and stomach from my mind.'

This resolution gave him a peculiar strength. He developed on those lines : 'If by avoiding food I should help the trees bloom, and the grass grow, why not do it thoroughly?' For the first time in his life he was making an earnest effort, for the first time he was learning the thrill of full application, outside money and love; for the first time he was doing a thing in which he was not personally interested. He felt suddenly so enthusiastic that it gave him a new strength to go through with the ordeal. The fourth day of his fast found him quite sprightly. He went down to the river, stood facing upstream with his eyes shut, and repeated the litany. It was no more than a supplication to the heavens to send down rain and save humanity. It was set in a certain rhythmic chant, which lulled his senses and awareness, so that as he went on saying it over and over again, the world around became blank. He nearly lost all sensation, except the numbness at his knees, through constant contact with cold water. Lack of food gave him a peculiar floating feeling, which he rather enjoyed, with the thought in the background, 'This enjoyment is something Velan cannot take away from me.'

The hum of humanity around was increasing. His awareness of his surroundings was gradually lessening in a sort of inverse proportion. He was not aware of it, but the world was beginning to press around. The pen of the wandering journalist had done the trick. Its repercussions were far and wide. The railways were the first to feel the pressure. They had to run special trains for the crowds that were going to Malgudi. People travelled on footboards and on the roofs of coaches. The little Malgudi Station was choked with passengers. Outside the station buses stood, the conductors crying, 'Special for Mangala leaving. Hurry up. Hurry up.' People rushed up from the station into the buses, and almost sat on top of each other. Gaffur's tax drove up and down a dozen times a day. And the crowd congregated around the river at Mangala. People sat in groups along its sand-bank, down its stones and steps, all the way up the opposite bank, wherever they could squeeze themselves in. Never had this part of the country seen such a crowd. Shops sprang up overnight, as if by magic, on bamboo poles roofed with thatch, displaying coloured soda bottles and bunches of bananas and coconut toffees. The Tea Propaganda Board opened a big tea stall, and its posters, green tea plantations along the slopes of blue mountains, were pasted all around the temple wall. (People drank too much coffee and too little tea in these parts.) They had put up a tea-bar and served free tea in porcelain cups all day. The public swarmed around it like flies, and the flies swarmed on all the cups and sugar bowls. The presence of the flies brought in the Health Department, who feared an outbreak of some epidemic in the crowded place without water. The khaki-clad health inspectors sprayed every inch of space with D.D.T. and, with needle in hand, coaxed people to innoculate themselves against cholera, malaria, and what not. A few youngsters just for fun bared their biceps, while a big crowd stood about and watched. There was a blank space in the rear wall of the temple where they cleaned up the ground and made a space for people to sit around and watch a film-show when it grew dark. They attracted people to it by playing popular film-hits on a gramophone with its loudspeakers mounted on the withering tree-tops. Men, women, and children crowded in to watch the film-shows, which were all about mosquitoes, malaria, plague, and tuberculosis, and B.C.G. vaccination. When a huge close-up of a mosquito was shown as the cause of malaria, a peasant was overheard saying, 'Such huge mosquitoes! No wonder the people get malaria in those countries. Our own mosquitoes are so tiny that they are harmless,' which depressed the lecturer on malaria so much that he remained silent for ten minutes. When he had done with health, he showed a few Government of India films about dams, river-valleys, and various projects, with Ministers delivering speeches. Far off, outside the periphery, a man had opened a gambling booth with a dartboard on a pole, and he had also erected a crude merry-go-around, which whined all day. Peddlers of various kinds were also threading in and out, selling balloons, reed-whistles, and sweets.

A large crowd always stood around and watched the Saint with profound awe. They touched the water at his feet and sprinkled it over their heads. They stood indefinitely around, until the master of the ceremonies, Velan, begged them to move. 'Please go away. The Swami must have fresh air. If you have had your *darshan*, move on and let others have theirs. Don't be selfish.' And then the people moved on, and enjoyed themselves in various ways. When the Swami went in to lie on his mat in the hall, they came in again to look at him, and stood about until Velan once again told them to keep moving. A few were specially privileged to sit on the edge of the mat very close to the great man. One of them was the schoolmaster, who took charge of all the telegrams and letters that were pouring in from all over the country wishing the Swami success. The post office at Mangala normally had a visiting postman coming once a week; and when a telegram came it was received at Aruna, a slightly bigger village seven miles down the river course, and was kept there until some-one could be found going to Mangala. But now the little telegraph office had no rest—day and night messages poured in just addressed, 'Swamiji'—that was all. They were piling up every hour and had to be sent down by special messengers. In addition to the arriving telegrams, there were many going out. The place was swarming with press reporters, who were rushing their hour-to hour stories to their papers all over the world. They were an aggressive lot and the little telegraph master was scared of them. They banged on his window and cried, 'Urgent.' They held out packets, and packed-up spools, and photographs, and ordered him to dispatch them at once. They cried, 'Urgent, urgent! If this packet does not reach my office today' and they threatened terrifying prospects and said all sorts of frightening things. 'Press. Urgent!' 'Press. Urgent!' They went on shouting till they reduced the man to a nervous wreck. He had promised his children that he would take them to see the Swamiji. The children cried, 'They are also showing an Ali Baba film, a friend told me.' But the man was given no time to fulfil his promise to his children. When the pressmen gave him respite, the keys rattled with incoming messages. He had spent a fairly peaceful life until then, and the present strain tore at his nerves. He sent off an S.O.S. to all his official superiors whenever he found breathing space. 'Handling two hundred messages today. Want relief—'

The roads were choked with traffic, country carts, buses and cycles, jeeps and automobiles of all kinds and ages. Pedestrians in files with hampers and baskets crossed the fields, like swarms of ants converging on a lump of sugar. The air rang with the music of a few who had chosen to help the Swami by sitting near him, singing devotional songs, to the accompaniment of a harmonium and *tabala*.

The busiest man here was an American, wearing a thin bush-shirt over corduroys. He arrived in a jeep with a trailer, dusty, rugged, with a mop of tousled hair, at about 1 p.m. on the tenth day of the fast and set himself to work immediately. He had picked up an interpreter at Madras and had driven straight through, three hundred and seventy-five miles. He pushed everything aside and took charge of the scene. He looked about only for a moment, driving his jeep down to the hibiscus bush behind the temple. He jumped off and strode past everyone to the pillared hall. He went up to the recumbent Swami, and brought his palms together, muttering '*Namaste*'—the Indian salute, which he had learnt the moment he landed in India. He had briefed himself on all the local manners. Raju looked on him with interest — the large, pink-faced arrival was a novel change in the routine. The pink visitor stooped low to ask the schoolmaster, sitting beside the Swami, 'Can I speak to him in English?'

'Yes. He knows Engligh.' The man lowered himself on to the edge of the mat and with difficulty sat down on the floor, Indian fashion, crossing his legs. He bent close to the Swami to say, 'I'm James J. Malone. I'm from California. My business is production of films and TV shows. I have come to shoot this subject, take it back to our country and show it to our people there. I have in my pocket the sanction from New Delhi for this project. May I have yours?'

Raju thought over it and serenely nodded.

'O.K. Thanks a lot. I won't disturb you—but will you let me shoot pictures of you? I wouldn't disturb you. Will it bother you if I move a few things up and fix the cable and lights'?

'No; you may do your work,' said the sage.

The man became extremely busy. He sprang to his feet, pulled the trailer into position and started his generator. Its throbbing filled the place, overwhelming all other noises. It brought in a huge crowed of men, women and children to watch the fun. All the other attractions in the camp became secondary. As Malone drew the cables about, a big crowd followed him. He grinned at them affably and went about his business. Velan and one or two others ran through the crowd crying, 'Is this a fish market? Get away all of you who have no work here!' But nobody was affected by his orders. They climbed pillars and pedestals and clung to all sorts of places to reach positions of vantage. Malone went on with his job without noticing anything. Finally, when he had the lights ready, he brought in his camera and took pictures of the people, the temple, and of the Swami from various angles and distances. 'I'm sorry, Swami, if the light is too strong.' When he had finished with the pictures, he brought in a microphone, put it near the Swami's face, and said, 'Let us chat. O.K.? Tell me, how do you like it here?'

'I am only doing what I have to do; that's all. My likes and dislikes do not count.'

'How long have you been without food now?'

'Ten days.'

'Do you feel weak?'

'Yes.'

'When will you break your fast?'

'Twelfth day.'

'Do you expect to have the rains by then?'

'Why not?'

'Can fasting abolish all wars and bring in world peace?'

'Yes.'

'Do you champion fasting for everyone?'

'Yes.'

'What about the caste system? Is it going?'

'Yes.'

'Will you tell us something about your early life?'

'What do you want me to say?'

'Er—for instance, have you always been a Yogi?'

'Yes; more or less.'

It was very hard for the Swami to keep up a continuous flow of talk. He felt exhausted and lay back. Velan and others looked on with concern. The schoolmaster said, 'He is fatigued.'

'Well, I guess we will let him rest for a while. I'm sorry to bother you.'

The Swami lay back with this eyes closed. A couple of doctors, deputed by the Government to watch and report, went to the Swami, felt his pulse and heart. They helped him to stretch himself on the mat. A big hush fell upon the crowd. Velan plied his fan more vigorously than ever. He looked distraught and unhappy. In fact, keeping a sympathetic fast, he was now eating on alternate days, confining his diet to saltless boiled greens. He looked worn out. He said to the master, 'One more day. I don't know how he is going to bear it. I dread to think how he can pull through another day.' Malone resigned himself to waiting. He looked at the doctor and asked, 'How do you find him?'

'Not very satisfactory; blood pressure is 200 systolic. We suspect one of the kidneys is affected. Uraemia is setting in. We are trying to give him small doses of saline and glucose. His life is valuable to the country.'

'Would you say a few words about his health,' Malone said, thrusting his microphone forward. He was sitting on the head of a carved elephant decorating the steps to the pillared hall. The doctors looked at each other in panic and said, 'Sorry. We are Government servants—we cannot do it without permission. Our reports are released only from headquarters. We cannot give them direct. Sorry.'

'Okay. I wouldn't hurt your customs.' He looked at his watch and said, 'I guess that's all for the day.' He approached the schoolmaster and said, "Tell me, what time does he step into the river tomorrow?'

'Six a.m.'

'Could you come over and show me the location?' The schoolmaster got up and took him along. The man said, 'Wait, wait. You'll not mind understudying for him for a minute. Show me where he starts from, how he goes up, and where he stops and stands.' The teacher hesitated, feeling too shy to understudy the sage. The man urged him on. 'Come on; be co-operative. I'll take care of it, if there is any trouble.' The teacher started from the pedestal. 'He starts here. Now follow me.' He showed the whole route down to the river, and the spot where the Swami would stop and pray, standing in water for two hours. The crowd followed keenly every inch of this movement, and someone in the crowd was joking, 'Oh! The master is also going to do penance and starve!' And they all laughed. Malone threw a smile at them from time to time, although he did not know what they were saying. He surveyed the place from various angles, measured the distance from the generator, shook the schoolmaster's hand,

and went back to his jeep. 'See you tomorrow morning.' He drove off amidst a great roar and puffing of his engine as his jeep rattled over the pits and ditches beyond the hibiscus, until he reached the road.

The eleventh day, morning. The crowd, pouring in all night, had nearly trebled itself because it was the last day of the fast. All night one could hear voices of people and the sound of vehicles rattling over the roads and pathways. Velan and a band of his assistants formed a cordon and kept the crowd out of the pillared hall. They said, 'The Swami must have fresh air to breathe. It's the only thing he takes now. Don't choke the air. Everyone can have *his darshan* at the river. I promise. Go away now. He is resting.' It was an all-night vigil. The numerous lanterns and lamps created a criss-cross of bewildering shadows on all hedges, trees and walls.

At five-thirty in the morning, the doctors examined the Swami. They wrote and signed a bulletin saying: 'Swami's condition grave. Declines glucose and saline. Should break the fast immediately. Advise procedure.' They sent a man running to send off his telegram to their headquarters. It was a Top Priority Government telegram, and it fetched a reply within an hour. 'Imperative that Swami should be saved. Persuade best to co-operate. Should not risk life. Try give glucose and saline. Persuade Swami resume fast later.'

They sat beside the Swami and read to him the message. He smiled at it. He beckoned Velan to come nearer. The doctors appealed, 'Tell him he should save himself. Please, do your best. He is very weak.' Velan bent close to the Swami and said, 'The doctors say—' In answer Raju asked the man to bend nearer, and whispered, 'Help me to my feet,' and clung to his arm and lifted himself. He got up to his feet. He had to be held by Velan and another on each side. In the profoundest silence the crowd followed him down. Everyone followed in a solemn, silent pace. The eastern sky was red. Many in the camp were still sleeping.

Raju could not walk, but he insisted upon pulling himself along all the same. He panted with the effort. He went down the steps of the river, halting for breath on each step, and finally reached his basin of water. He stepped into it, shut his eyes and turned towards the mountain, his lips muttering the prayer. Velan and another held him each by an arm. The morning sun was out by now; a great shaft of light illuminated the surroundings. It was difficult to hold Raju on his feet, as he had a tendency to flop down. They held him as if he were a baby. Raju opened his eyes, looked about, and said, 'Velan, it's raining in the hills. I can feel it coming up under my feet, up my legs—' and with that he sagged down.

(From *The Guide*, Indian Thought Publication, Mysore)

Leela's Friend

Sidda was hanging about the gate at a moment when Mr Sivasanker was standing in the front veranda of his house, brooding over the servant problem.

'Sir, do you want a servant?' Sidda asked.

'Come in,' said Mr Sivasanker. As Sidda opened the gate and came in Mr Sivasanker subjected him to a scrutiny and said to himself, 'Doesn't seem to be a bad sort ... At any rate the fellow looks tidy.' 'Where were you before?' he asked.

Sidda said, 'In a bunglow there,' and indicated a vague somewhere 'in the doctor's house.'

'What is his name?'

'I don't know, master?' Sidda said. 'He lives near the market.'

'Why did they send you away?'

'They left the town, master.' Sidda said, giving the stock reply.

Leela's Friend

Mr Sivasanker asked, 'What sort of work can you do?'

'Anything, master. I will do anything I am asked to do.'

Mr Sivasanker was unable to make up his mind. He called his wife. She looked at him and said. 'He doesn't seem to me worse than the others we have had...' Leela, their five-year-old daughter, came out, looked at Sidda, and gave a cry of joy 'Oh father!' she said, 'I like him. Don't send him away. Let us keep him in our house.' And that decided it.

Sidda was given two meals a day and four rupees a month, in return for which he washed clothes, tended the garden, ran errands, chopped wood and looked after Leela.

'Sidda, come and play!' Leela would cry, and Sidda had to drop any work he might be doing, and ran to her, as she stood in the front garden with a red ball in her hand. His company made her supremely happy. She flung the ball at him and he flung it back. And then she said, 'Now throw the ball into the sky.' Sidda clutched the ball, closed his eyes for a second, and threw the ball up. When the ball came down again, he said, 'Now this has touched the moon and come. You see here a little bit of the moon sticking.' Leela keenly examined the ball for traces of the moon and said, 'I don't see it.'

'You must be very quick about it,' said Sidda, 'because it will all evaporate and go back to the moon. Now hurry up...' He covered the ball tightly with his fingers and allowed her to peep through a little gap.

'Ah, yes,' said Leela. 'I see the moon, but is the moon very wet?'

'Certainly, it is,' Sidda said.

'What is in the sky, Sidda?'

'God,' he said.

'If we stand on the roof and stretch our arm, can we touch the sky?'

'Not if we stand on the roof here,' he said. 'But if you stand on coconut tree you can touch the sky.'

'Have you done it?' asked Leela.

'Yes, many times,' said Sidda. 'Whenever there is a big moon, I climb a coconut tree and touch it.'

'Does the moon know you?'

'Yes, very well. Now come with me. I will show you something nice.' They were standing near the rose plant. He said, pointing, 'You see the moon there, don't you?'

'Yes.'

'Now come with me,' he said and took her to the backyard. He stopped near the well, and pointed up. The moon was there too. Leela clapped her hands and screamed in wonder, 'The moon here! It was there! How is it?'

'I have asked it to follow us about.'

Leela ran in and told her mother, 'Sidda knows the moon.' At dusk he carried her in and she held a class for him. She had a box filled with catalogues, illustrated books and stumps of pencils. It gave her great joy to play the teacher to Sidda. She made him squat on the floor with a pencil between his fingers and a catalogue in front of him. She had another pencil and a catalogue and commanded. 'Now write.' And he had to try and copy whatever she wrote in the pages of her catalogue. She knew two or three letters in the alphabet and could draw a kind of cat and crow. But none of these Sidda could copy even remotely. She said, examining his effort. 'Is this how I have drawn the crow? Is this how I have drawn the "B"?' She pitied him and redoubled her efforts to teach him. But that good fellow, though an adept at controlling the moon, was utterly incapable of plying the pencil. Consequently, it looked as though Leela would keep him there pinned to his seat till his stiff, inflexible wrist cracked. He sought relief by saying, 'I think your mother is calling you in to dinner.' Leela would drop the pencil and run out of the room and the school hour would end. After dinner Leela ran to her bed. Sidda had to be ready with a story. He sat down on the floor near the bed and told incomparable stories: of animals in the jungles, of gods in heaven, of magicians who could conjure up golden castles and fill them with little princesses and their pets...

Day by day she clung to him closer. She insisted upon having his company all her waking hours. She was at his side when he was working in the garden or chopping wood, and accompanied him when he was sent on errands.

One evening he went out to buy sugar and Leela went with him. When they came home, Leela's mother noticed that a gold chain Leela had been wearing was missing. 'Where is your chain?' she asked. Leela looked into her shirt, searched and said, 'I don't know.' Her mother gave her a slap and said, 'How many times have I told you to take it off and put it in the box?' 'Sidda, Sidda!' she shouted a moment later. As Sidda came in Leela's mother threw up a glance at him and thought the fellow already looked queer. She asked him about the chain. His throat went dry. He blinked and answered that he did not know. She mentioned the police and shouted at him. She had to go back into the kitchen for a moment because she had left something on the oven. Leela followed her whinning, 'Give me some sugar, mother, I am hungry.' When they came out again and called. 'Sidda, Sidda!' there was no answer. Sidda had vanished into the night.

Mr Sivasanker came home an hour later, grew very excited over all this, went to the police station and lodged with them a complaint.

After food Leela refused to go to bed. 'I won't sleep unless Sidda comes and tells me stories.... I don't like you mother, You are always abusing and worrying Sidda.... Why are you so rough?'

'But he has taken away your chain...'

'Let him. It doesn't matter. Tell me a story.'

'Sleep, sleep.' said mother, attempting to make her lie down on her lap.

'Tell me a story, mother,' Leela said. It was utterly impossible for her mother to think of a story now. Her mind was too much disturbed. The thought of Sidda made her panicky. The fellow, with his knowledge of the household, might come in at night and loot. She shuddered to think what a villain she had been harbouring all these days. It was God's mercy that he hadn't killed the child for the chain. . . . 'Sleep, Leela, sleep,' she cabled.

'Can't you tell the story of the elephant?' Leela asked.

'No.'

Leela made a noise of deprecation and asked. 'Why should not Sidda sit in our chair, mother?' Mother didn't answer the question. Leela said a moment later, 'Sidda is gone because he wouldn't be allowed to sleep inside the house just as we do. Why should he always be made to sleep outside the house, mother? I think he is angry with us, mother.'

By the time Sivasanker returned Leela had slept. He said 'What a risk we took in engaging that fellow. It seems he is an old criminal. He has been in jail half a dozen times for stealing jewellery on children. In a moment (from the description I gave) the Inspector was able to identify him.'

'Where is he now?' asked the wife.

'The police know his haunts. They will pick him up very soon, don't worry. The Inspector was furious that I didn't consult him before employing him...'

Four days later, just as father was coming home from office, a Police Inspector and a constable brought in Sidda. Sidda stood with bowed head. Leela was overjoyed. 'Sidda! Sidda!' she cried and ran down the steps to meet him.

'Don't go near him,' the Inspector said, stopping her.

'Why not?'

'He is a thief. He has taken away your gold chain.'

'Let him. I will have a new chain.' Leela said, and all of them laughed. And then Mr Sivasanker spoke to Sidda; and then his wife addressed him a few words on his treachery. They then

Leela's Friend

asked him where he had kept the chain.

'I have not taken it,' Sidda said feebly, looking at the ground.

'Why did you run away without saying so?' asked Leela's mother. There was no answer.

Leela's face became red. 'Oh, policemen, leave him alone. I want to play with him.'

'My dear child,' said the Police Inspector. 'He is a thief?'

'Let him be,' Leela replied haughtily.

'What a devil you must be to steal a thing from such an innocent child!' remarked the Inspector. 'Even now it is not too late. Return it. I will let you off provided you promise not to do such a thing again.' Leela's father and mother too joined in this appeal. Leela felt disgusted with the whole business and said. 'Leave him alone, he hasn't taken the chain.'

'You are not at all a safe prosecution witness, my child,' observed the Inspector humorously.

'No, he hasn't taken it!' Leela screamed.

Her father said, 'Baby, if you don't behave, I will be very angry with you.'

Half an hour later the Inspector said to the constable, 'Take him to the station. I think I shall have to sit up with him tonight.' The constable held Sidda by the hand and turned to go. Leela ran behind them crying. 'Don't take him. Leave him here, leave him here.' She clung to Sidda's hand. He looked at her mutely, like an animal. Mr Sivasanker went up and carried Leela back into the house. Leela was in tears.

Everyday when Mr Sivasanker came home he was asked by his wife. 'Any news of the jewel?' and by his daughter, 'Where is Sidda?'

'They still have him in the lockup though he is very stubborn and won't say anything about the jewel.' said Mr Sivasanker. 'Bah! What a rough fellow he must be!' said his wife with a shiver.

'Oh, these fellows who have been in jail once or twice lose all fear. Nothing can make them confess.'

A few days later, putting her hand into the tamarind pot in the kitchen, Leela's mother picked up the chain. She took it to the tap and washed off the coating of tamarind on it. It was unmistakably the old chain. When it was shown to her, Leela said, 'Give it here. I want to wear the chain.'

'How did it get into the tamarind pot?' mother asked.

'Somehow,' replied Leela.

'Did you put it in?' asked mother.

'Yes.'

'When?'

'Long ago, the other day.'

'Why didn't you say so before?'

'I don't know,' said Leela.

When father came home and was told, he said, 'The child must not have any chain hereafter. Didn't I tell you that I saw her carrying it in her hand once or twice? She must have dropped it into the pot sometime.... And all this bother on account of her.'

'What about Sidda?' asked mother.

'I will tell the Inspector tomorrow.... In any case, we couldn't have kept a criminal like him in the house...'

(From *Lawley Road*, Orient Paperbacks, Delhi)

7. RAJA RAO

Born in 1909 in Hassan, a village in Karnataka, Raja Rao was educated at Hyderabad and Aligarh. He went for higher studies to Montpellier and Sorbonne in France where he came to live for nearly thirty years before joining the University of Texas, Austin (USA) as Professor of Philosophy. Though he has genuine fondress for America, he feels his roots are in India and visits this country frequently.

Raja Rao is the most individualistic of Indian creative writers in English and the most conscious of the dignity of his vocation. His first novel, *Kanthapura* (1938), was hailed by E.M. Forster as the finest of its kind about India that had appeared till then. His first collection of short stories, *The Cow of the Barricades and Other Stories*, was published in 1947. Thirteen Years later appeared his most ambitious and mature work, *The Serpent and the Rope*, which won him the Sahitya Akademi Award in 1966 and Padma Bhushan in 1969. It was followed by *The Cat and Shakespeare, A Tale of Modern India* (1965). An English translation of an earlier work of his in French novel, *Comrade Kirillov*, appeared in 1976. Raja Rao is at present completing a novel about India and America called *The Chessmaster and His Moves*.

Raja Rao, through his experiments with language and form, has given the Indo-Anglian novel a distinctly Indian character and a subject matter that brings out the characteristic Indian preoccupation with metaphysical questions.

Kanthapura, one of the most remarkable Indian novels in English, brings out the social and political concerns which Raja Rao shared with other Indian writers of the thirties. Kanthapura, an imaginary south Indian village, becomes symbolic of a resurgent India as it responds to Mahatma Gandhi's call for non-cooperation. Critics have described the novel as a kind of *Sthala-Purana*, 'Tale of a Place,' which is an apt description of its content and technique. The village itself with its temple of the Goddess Kenchamma becomes the point of convergence for the three main movements dealt with in the novel: the religious, the political and the social.

At the centre of the novel is Moorthy, a true humanitarian steeped in the tradition and thought of Mahatma Gandhi. Referred to as the 'saint of our village' and 'our Gandhi,' Moorthy awakens the social and political consciousness of the close-knit rural community of Kanthapura. The villagers organise a volunteer corps and celebrate religious festivals aimed at creating a spirit of service to the community and a sense of commitment to the achievement of India's political freedom. Moorthy receives great support from men and women of the various social strata in Kanthapura. However, Bhatta, a self-centred man, will have nothing to do with Gandhi bhajans started by Moorthy. Bhatta opposes Moorthy's attempts to bring about the emancipation of the rural community and even joins hands with Bade Khan, the policeman of the Skeffington Coffee Estate, in oppressing the poor. This estate, owned by the Red-man (Englishman) who exploits the poor Indian coolies, symbolises the oppressive role of British commercialism in India.

The crudity and vulgarity of the Red-man and the barbarity of Bade Khan cast a shadow on the life of the plain and simple folk of Kanthapura. Bhatta, too, adds his share to their suffering. He is an unworthy man, a bad husband, a greedy person and an oppressor of Narasamma, the coolie. His superficial god-fearing sentiment is exposed by his desire to go to Benares (Varanasi) to wash away his sins. But it is the atrocities of the policemen that spell disaster in Kanthapura and bring about its desolation. All houses are deserted, the people having fled. Only one person Range Gowda, returns to Kanthapura, but as a 'broken man'. The novel, thus ends on a note of desolation. 'But to tell you the truth, mother, my heart, it beat like a drum,' comments the author.

In chapters 5 and 6 the Skeffington Coffee Estate and the hilly area around it are described. The workers are exploited by the owner of the estate and even caned by the maistri. There is naked exploitation of these helpless people—economic as well as sexual. The Red-man's rapacity and sensuality is seen in his shooting Seetharam, one of the workers, when he refuses to give his daughter, Mira to him. Bade Khan allows himself to be used as the Red-man's instrument of oppression. Moorthy leads a protest march of the workers against the owner, and tries to enter the gate of the Coffee Estate. He is obstructed by Bade Khan. Vasudev and other workers lead Moorthy away from the Estate to Kanthapura. Bade Khan whips Radhanna, another worker, and his wife and drives them out of their dwelling. They go to Kanthapura and seek refuge there. This marks the beginning of Moorthy's 'Don't-touch-the-Government Campaign.'

What follows (chapter 7-8) is an account of Moorthy and the men and women of Kanthapura and their involvement in a movement of emancipation:

Kanthapura

And this is how it all began. That evening Moorthy speaks to Rangamma on the veranda and tells her he will fast for three days in the temple, and Rangamma says, 'What for, Moorthy?' and Moorthy says that much violence had been done because of him, and that were he full of the radiance of ahimsa such things should never have happened, but Rangamma says, 'That was not your fault, Moorthy!' to which he replies, 'The fault of others, Rangamma, is the fruit of one's own disharmony,' and silently he walks, down the steps, and walks up to the temple, where, seated beside the central piller of the mandap, he begins to meditate. And when the evening meal is over Rangamma comes to find our Seenu, and lantern in hand and with a few bananas in her sari fringe, she goes to the temple, and Moorthy, when he sees the light, smiles and asks what it is all about. Rangamma simply places the bananas before him and stands waiting for a word from him. Moorthy lifts up the bananas and says, 'I will drink but three cups of salted water each day, and that I shall procure myself. I shall go to the river and get water, and tomorrow if you can get me a handful of salt, that is all I ask.'

At this Rangamma lets fall a tear, and Seenu, who has been silent and has been looking away toward the sanctum and the idols and the candelabras and the flowers, turns towards Moorthy and says, 'No, Moorthy, this is all very well for the Mahatma, but not for us poor creatures,' to which Moorthy answers calmly, 'Never mind—let me try. I will not die of it, will I?' And Rangamma says this and Seenu says that, and there is no end to the song. Then Ramakrishnayya himself comes to take Rangamma away and he says, 'Let the boy do what he likes, Ranga. If he wants to rise lovingly to God and burn the dross of the flesh through vows, it is not for us sinners to say "Nay, nay",' and after a hurried circumambulation of the temple, they go down the promontory and hurry back home.

Moorthy said his *gayatri* thrice a thousand and eight times, and when the sanctum lights began to flicker he spread out his upper cloth on the floor and laid himself down. Sleep slowly came over him, and so deep was his rest that pepole were already moving about in streets when he awoke. He rose quickly and hurried down to the river and hurried back again and, seated by the central pillar, began once more to meditate. People came and people went; they banged the bell and touched the bull and took the flowers, and still did Moorthy enter deeper and deeper into meditation; and it was only Waterfall Venkamma who roused him with her loud laughter: 'Ah, the cat has begun to take to asceticism,' says she, 'only to commit more sins. He, son! when did you begin to lie to your neighbours? As though it were not enough to have polluted our village with your Pariahs! Now you want to pollute us with your gilded purity! Wait! Wait! When you come out of this counting of beads, I shall give you a fine welcome with my broomstick!' But as Moorthy does not move, she puts her hand into her clothes-basket, and taking out a wet roll of sari, she holds it over his head and squeezes it. 'This is an oblation to thee, Pariah!' says she, and as she sees Rangamma's sister, Seethamma, drawing near, she laughs at Moorthy and laughs again, and then she jabbers and shouts and goes away, still chattering to herself. Moorthy loosens his limbs and, holding his breath, says to himself, 'I shall love even my enemies. The Mahatma says he would love even our enemies,' and closing his eyes, tighter, he slips back into the foldless sheath of the soul, and sends out rays of love to the east, rays of love to the west, rays of love to the north, rays of love to the south, and love to the earth below and to the sky above, and he feels such exaltation creeping into his limbs and head that his heart begins to beat out a song, and the song of Kabir comes into his mind:

The road to the city of love is hard, brother,
Its hard,
Take care, take care, as you walk along it,

Singing this his exaltation grows and grows, and tears come to his eyes. And when he opens them to look round, a great blue radiance seems to fill the whole earth, and, dazzled, he rises up and falls prostrate before the god, chanting Sankara's 'Sivoham, Sivoham. I am Siva. I am Siva. Siva am I.'

Then he sat himself down by the central pillar and slipped back into meditation. Why was it he could meditate so deeply? Thoughts seemed to ebb away to the darkened shores and leave the illumined consciousness to rise up into the back of the brain, he had explained to Seenu. Light seemed to rise from the far horizon, converge and creep over hills and fields and trees, and rising up the promontory, infuse itself through his very toes and finger tips and rise to the sun-centre of his heart. There was a vital softness about it he had hardly ever felt. Once, however, in childhood he had felt that vital softness—once, as he was seated by the river, while his mother was washing the clothes, and the soft leap of the waters over smooth boulders so lulled him to quiet that he closed his eyes, and his closed eyes led him to say his prayers, and he remembered the child Prahlada who had said Hari was everywhere, and he said to himself, 'I shall see Hari, too,' and he had held his breath hushed, and the beating of the clothes sank into his ears, and the sunshine sank away into his mind, and his limbs sank down into the earth, and then there was a dark burning light in the heart of the sanctum, and many men with beards and besmeared with holy ashes stood beside the idol, silent, their lips gently moving, and he, too, entered the temple like a sparrow, and he sat on a handle of the candelabra, and as he looked fearfully at the holy, floods suddenly swept in from all the doorways of the temple, beating, whirling floods, dark and bright, and he quietly sank into them and floated away like child Krishna on the pipal leaf. But it was so bright everywhere that he opened his eyes and he felt so light and airy that his mother looked near and small like one at the foot of a hill. And up there over the mountains there was nothing but light and that cool, blue-spreading light had entered his limbs. And that very evening he said to his mother, 'Mother, now you can throw me down the mountains,' and she asked, 'Why, my son?' and he answered, 'Why, mother, because Hari will fly down and hold me in his arms as I roll down the mountains. And if you send elephants to kill me, the elephants will stand by and say, "This is Hari's child," and lift me up with their trunks and seat me on their backs and throw a garland round my neck. And the poison you will give me in the cup of death will become the water of flowers, for, Mother, I have seen Hari...'

The next time he felt like that was when he had those terrible floods, and he had, he told us later, seated himself by the river and said, 'I may be drowned, but I shall not rise, Mother Himavathy, till thy waters are sunk down to thy daily shores.' And who will say the waters did not sink back that very evening? But no other such vision of the holy had he till that holy vision of the Mahatma.

But this morning his soul sounded deeper still. Why?—he began to ask himself. No answer came, but he merged deeper into himself and radiance poured out of his body and he seemed to rise sheer into the air. He floated and floated in it, and he felt he could fly so far and so free that he felt a terror strike his being and, suddenly perspiring, he drew his soul back to the earth, and, opening his eyes touched his limbs and felt his face and hit the floor to feel he was alive. But he had caught a little of that primordial radiance, and through every breath more and more love seemed to pour out of him.

That was why, when Ratna came to see him, he felt there was something different in his feelings toward her. Her smile did not seem to touch his heart with delicate satisfaction as it did before. She seemed something so feminine and soft and distant, and the idea that he could ever think of her other than as a sister shocked him and sent a shiver down his spine. But Ratna looked at him sadly and shyly, and whispered, 'Is there anything I can do?'

and Moorthy answered, 'Pray with me that the sins of others may be purified with our prayers.' She could hardly grasp his idea. She was but fifteen. Praying seemed merely to fall flat before the gods in worship. So she said she would make ten more prostrations before the gods, and when her mother came along, she stood silent, and once Seethamma had finished her circumambulations, they smiled to Moorthy and walked back home.

Rangamma came as the cattle were being driven to the fields, and she brought with her a handful of salt. Moorthy poured a little water into his tumbler, and throwing in a pinch of salt, swallowed it all, crying, 'Rama-Krishna, Rama-Krishna.' But the coolness in his empty stomach made him shiver. Then a warmth rose in his veins and he felt strength streaming into his limbs. Rangamma again tried to persuade him to eat a little— 'Just not to be too weak, for even the *dharma sastras* permit it,' she said. But Moorthy had little strength to answer her, and he simply smiled back, saying, 'Nay.' And when she came back in the evening there were already around Moorthy, Pariah Rachanna and Beadle Timmayya and Patel Range Gowda, and Dore, who had just come back from one of his tours. And Dore laughed and mocked at Moorthy, saying it was not for a university fellow to play all these grandma's tricks. But they silenced him. And then there were also there the other boys Kittu and Ramu and Postmaster's Seetharamu and our Seenu and Devaru's son, Subbu, and Moorthy sat among them smiling and calm, saying a word now and again. But strength was going out of his breath and his face began to grow shiny and shrivelled, and when dusk fell they all left him, and it was only Rangamma that went to sit near him for one moment in silence. 'The great enemy is in us, Rangamma,' said Moorthy, slowly, 'hatred is in us. If only we could not hate, if only we would show fearless, calm affection toward our fellow men, we would be stronger, and not only would the enemy yield, but he would be converted. If I, I alone, could love Bade Khan, I am sure our cause would win. Maybe—I shall love him—with your blessings!' Rangamma did not understand this, neither, to tell you the truth, did any of us. We would do harm to no living creature. But to love Bade Khan—no, that was another thing. We would not insult him. We would not hate him. But we could not love him. How could we? He was not my uncle's son, was he? And even if he were....

The next day Moorthy was weaker still. But Bhatta, furious that Moorthy was pretending to be pious, tried to talk to him, and when Moorthy, smiling, just said, 'Bhattare, I am weak: I shall explain this to you another time,' Bhatta insulted him and swore he would beat the drum and denounce this cat's conversion to asceticism. But Moorthy simply smiled back again, for love was growing in him.

On the third day such exaltation came over him that he felt blanketed with the Pariah and the cur. He felt he could touch the stones and they would hang to his hands, he felt he could touch a snake and it would spread its sheltering hood above him. But as he rose he felt such a dizziness enter his head that he had to hold to the wall to move, and when he sat down after the morning prayers he felt his heart beating itself away. His eyes dimmed and the whole temple seemed to shake and sink, and the fields rose up with crops and canals and all stood in the air while the birds seemed to screech in desolation. And as he lay back on his mat, a languor filled his limbs and he felt the earth beneath him quaking and splitting. When he awoke he saw Rangamma and our Seenu and Ratna all in tears, and he moved his head and asked, 'What's all this?' and Rangamma, so happy that he had at last awakened from his swoon, smiled back at him and said there was nothing the matter, and as he turned toward the courtyard he saw Pariah Rachanna and Lingayya standing with joined palms. Something was the matter, thought Moorthy, and holding to the pillar he slowly sat up, and he saw the sunshine flooding through the valley, while the bulls and buffaloes were husking paddy by the haystacks, and the canal water ran muddy as ever, and up the Bebbur mound the empty footpath, quivering in the heat, ran up into the Skeffington Coffee Estate. Then suddenly he broke into a fit of sobs, and they stood round him and asked, 'What's the matter? What?' and Moorthy would not answer. For somewhere behind the dizzy blare was a shadow that seemed to wail like an ominous crow, and he broke into sobs in spite of himself. Then Rangamma took an orange from her sari-hem and offered it to Moorthy imploringly and Moorthy looked at it distraught.

'An orange. This is an orange, Rangamma. And I cannot eat an orange.' he said, and Rangamma thought, 'Well, he has lost his reason.' But Moorthy grew calmer, and he said, 'Give me a little salted water. There is river water in this pot.' And as they gave it to him, he held the tumbler long in his hands, and then slowly lifting it up to his lips, he drank one gulp, then another, and then another, and at each sip he seemed to feel light coming to his eyes, and such perspiration poured out from him that he laid himself down and covered himself gently, and sank back to sleep, and Rangamma said to Ratna, 'Sit in the courtyard, my daughter, and watch when he wakes. I have to go and cook.' At which Ratna was so happy and so proud that she sat by the bull and began to pray. 'God, God,' she said, 'Keep him strong and virtuous, and may he rise out of this holier and greater; God, I shall offer ten coconuts and a kumkum worship. God, keep him alive for me.' Then she rose and fell prostrate before the gods in the sanctum.

By the evening, the critical period being over, Moorthy felt stronger and he said to Rangamma, 'Rangamma, if we had a bhajan this evening?' and Rangamma said, 'But Moorthy, you are weak' —to which Moorthy replied, 'No, I'm weak no more. And if I am weak, Seenu will lead the bhajan.' And as dusk fell, Seenu lighted the oil lamps of the sanctum, and going up the promontory he rang the bell and blew the conch, and men came from the Potters' street and the Brahmins' street and the Weavers' street and the Pariah street; but Vasudev and Gangadhar were the only ones to come from the Skeffngton Coffee Estate. But later, Bade Khan came, too, to join them.

When the bhajan was over and Seenu was taking round the camphor censer, Moorthy observed how poor the Brahmin corner was. Neither Patwari Nanjundia nor Temple Nanjappa nor Schoolmaster Devarayya were there, nor their wives nor their children. The short, round picture of Bhatta came to his mind, but he put it away and thought of God. He would send out love where there was hatred and compassion where there was misery. Victory to the Mahatma!

A peace so vital entered his soul that the radiance of the earth filled him till the soul shone like an oleander at dawn.

The next morning he broke the fast, and lighter in limb and lighter in soul, he walked out to preach the 'Don't-touch the-Government' campaign.

First he goes to see Range Gowda. Nothing can be done without Range Gowda. When Range Godwa says, 'Yes,' you will have elephants and howdahs and music processions. If Range Gowda says 'No,' you can eat the bitter neem leaves and lie by the city gates, licked by the curs. That's how it is with our Range Gowda.

'Range Gowda, Range Gowda,' says Moorthy, 'there's something I want of you.'

'Come in, learned one, and, seated like a son, explain to me what you need. If there's anything this fool can do, do but open your mouth and it shall be done.'

And seated on the veranda, Moorthy explains to Range Gowda his program. Things are getting bad in the village. The Brahmins who were with him for the bhajans are now getting fewer and fewer. Some people have gone about threatening the community with the Swami's ex-communication, and people are afraid. There is Waterfall Venkamma and Temple Rangappa and Patwari Nanjundia and Schoolmaster Devarayya—and then, of course, there's Bhatta and when Bhatta's name is mentioned, Range Gowda's neck stiffens and spitting across the veranda to the gutter, he says, 'Yes, he had come to see me too.'

'To you, Range Gowda?'

'Yes, learned Moorthappa. He had, of course, come to see me. He wanted me to be his dog's tail. But I said to him, the Mahatma is a holy man, and I was not with the jackals but with the deer. At which Bhatta grew so furious that he cried out that this holy man was a tiger in a deer's skin, and said this about pollution and that about corruption, and I said to him, 'So it may be, but the Red-man's Government is no swan in a Himalayan lake.' Bhatta grew fierce again and said, 'We shall eat mud and nothing but mud.' 'Yes,' says I, 'if every bloke eats mud, I, too, shall eat mud. The laws of God are not made one for Range Gowda and one for Putte Gowda. Mud shall I eat, if mud I should eat.' And Range Gowda chuckles and spits, and munches on.

Then Moorthy says, 'This is what is to be done. We shall start a Congress group in Kanthapura, and the Congress group of Kanthapura will join the Congress of All India. You just pay four annas or two thousands yards of yarn per year, and that is all you have to do, and then you become a Congress member. And you must vow to speak truth, and wear no cloth but the khadi cloth.'

'Oh yes, Moorthappa! If you think there is no danger in it, I see no objection to joining it. Tell me only one thing: Will it bring us into trouble with the Government.'

This Moorthy thinks over and then he says, 'This is how it is, Range Gowda. Today it will bring us into no trouble with the Government. But tomorrow when we shall be against the Red-man's Government it will bring us into trouble. You see Bade Khan is already here...'

'Ah!' says Range Gowda. 'And I shall not close my eyes till that dog has eaten filth.' but Moorthy interrupts him and says such things are not to be said, and that hatred should be plucked out of our hearts, and that the Mahatma says you must love even your enemies.

'That's for the Mahatma and you, Moorthappa—not for us poor folk! When that cur Puttayya slipped through the night and plastered up the drain and let all the canal water into his fields and let mine get baked up in the sun, do you think kind words would go with him? Two slaps and he spits and he grunts, but he will never do that again.'

'That must not be done, Range Gowda. Every enemy you create is like pulling out a lantana bush in your back yard. The more you pull out, the wider you spread the seeds, and the thicker becomes the lantana growth. But every friend you create is like a jasmine hedge. You plant it, and it is there and bears flowers and you offer them to the gods, and the gods give them back to you and your women put them into their hair. Now, you see, you hit Puttayya and Puttayya goes and speaks of it to Madanna, and Madanna to Timmanna, and Puttayya and Timmanna and Madanna will hold vengefulness against you and some day this vengefulness will break forth in fire. But had you reasoned it out with Puttayya, maybe you would have come to an agreement, and your canal water would go to your fields, and his canal water to his fields.'

'Learned master, at this rate I should have to go and bow down to every Pariah and butcher and, instead of giving them a nice licking with my lantana switch, I should offer flowers and coconuts and betel leaves in respect and say, "Pray plough this field thiswise, maharaja! Pray plough this field that-wise, maharaja!" And I should not howl at my wife and let my son-in-law go fooling with Concubine Siddi's daughter, Mohini, who's just come of age. No, learned master, that is not just.'

'It's a long story, Range Gowda, and we shall speak of it another time. But you are a father of many children and an esteemed elder of your community and of the whole village, and if you should take to the ways of the Congress, then others will follow you.'

'But, learned master, there's nothing in common between what you were saying and this.'

'Most certainly, Range Gowda. One cannot become a member of the Congress if one will not promise to practice ahimsa, and to speak truth and to spin at least two thousand yards of yarn per year.' At which Range Gowda bursts out laughing again and says, 'Then I too will have one day to sit and meditate, taking three cups of salted water per day!' and Moorthy laughs with him, and once they have talked over rents and law courts and the sloth of the peasants, Range Gowda turns back to the subject and says, 'Do what you like, learned master. You know things better than I do, and I, I know you are not a man to spit on our confidence in you. If you think I should become a member of the Congress, let me be a member of the Congress. If you want me to be a slave, I shall be your slave. All I know is that what you told me about the Mahatma is very fine, and the Mahatma is a holy man, and if the Mahatma says what you say, let the Mahatma's word be the word of God. And if this buffalo will trample on it, may my limbs get paralysed and my tongue dumb and my progeny be forever destroyed?' Then Moorthy stands up and says it is no light matter to be a member of the Congress and that every promise before the Congress is a promise before the Mahatma and God, and Range Gowda interrupts him, saying, 'Of course, of course. And this Range Gowda has a golden tongue and a leather tongue, and what is uttered by the golden tongue is golden and sure, and what is uttered by the leather one is for the thief and concubine,' and Moorthy says, 'May the Mahatma's blessings be with us' and hurrying down the steps, he slips round to the Weavers' street, goes straight to the Weavers' elder, Ramayya, and he says, 'Rammayya, will you be a member of the panchayat of all India?'; and Ramayya asks, 'And what's that, learned one?' and Moorthy sits down and explains it, and Ramayya says, 'Oh, if the patel is with you, the panchayat is with him,' and Moorthy says, 'Then I'll go. I've still to see Potters' elder, Siddayya.' And Potters' elder, Siddayya, when he hears of the Mahatma and the patel, says, 'Of course, I'm with the patel and the panchayat,' and then Moorthy thinks, 'Now, this is going well,' and rushes down the Pariah quarter to see Rachanna. But Rachanna is out mowing at the river-eaten field, and Rachanna's wife is pounding rice, and she says, 'Come and sit inside, learned one, since you are one of us, for the sun is hot outside,' and Moorthy, who had never entered a Pariah house—he had always spoken to the Pariahs from the gutter-slab—Moorthy thinks this is something new, and with one foot to the back and one foot to the fore, he stands trembling and undecided, and then suddenly hurries up the steps and crosses the threshold and squats on the earthen floor. But Rachanna's wife quickly sweeps a corner, and spreads for him a wattle mat, but Moorthy, confused, blurts out, 'No, no, no, no,' and he looks this side and that and thinks surely there is a carcass in the back yard, and it's surely being skinned, and he smells the stench of hide and the stench of pickled pigs, and the room seems to shake, and all the gods and all the manes of heaven seem to cry out against him and his hands steal mechanically to the holy thread, and holding it, he feels he would like to say, 'Hari-Om, Hari-Om.' But Rachanna's wife has come back with a little milk in a shining brass tumbler, and placing it on the floor with stretched hands, she says, 'Accept this from this poor hussy!' and slips back behind the corn-bins; and Moorthy says, 'I've just taken coffee, Lingamma...' but she interrupts him and says, 'Touch it, Moorthappa, touch it only as though it were offered to the gods, and we shall be sanctified'; and Moorthy, with many a trembling prayer, touches the tumbler and brings it to his lips, and taking one sip, lays it aside.

Meanwhile Rachanna's two grandchildren come in, and gazing at Moorthy, they run into the back yard, and then Madanna's children come, and then Madanna's wife, pestle in hand, and

Madanna's wife's sister and her two-months-old brat in her arms, and then all the women and all the children of the Pariah quarter come and sit in Rachanna's central veranda and they all gaze silently at Moorthy, as though the sacred eagle had suddenly appeared in the heavens. Then Moorthy feels this is the right moment to talk, and straightening his back, he raises his head and says, 'Sisters, from today onward I want your help. There is a huge panchayat of all India called the Congress, and that Congress belongs to the Mahatma, and the Mahatma says every village in this country must have a panchayat like that, and everybody who will become a member of that panchayat will spin and practice ahimsa and speak the truth.' At this Rachanna's wife says, 'And what will it give us, learned one?' and Moorthy says something about the foreign Government and the heavy taxations and the poverty of the peasants, and they all say, 'Of course, of course,' and then he says, 'I ask you: will you spin a hundred yards of yarn per day?' But Madanna's wife says, 'I'm going to have a child,' and Satanna's wife says, 'I',m going for my brothers' marriage,' and her sister says, 'I'll spin if it will bring money. I don't want cloth like Timmayya and Madayya get with all their turning of the wheel,' and Chennayya's daughter says, 'I shall spin, learned master, I shall spin. But I shall offer my cloth to the Mahatma when he comes here,' at which all the women laugh and say, 'Yes, the Mahatma will come here to see your pretty face,' and the children who had climbed on the rice-sacks cry out, 'I too will turn the rattle, Master, I too.' And Moorthy feels this is awful, and nothing could be done with these women; so standing up, he asks, 'Is there no one among you who can spin a hundred yards of yarn per day?' And from this corner and that voices rise and Moorthy says, 'Then come forward and tell me if you can take an oath before the goddess that you will spin at least a hundred yards of yarn per day,' and they all cry out, 'No oath before the goddess! if we don't keep it, who will bear her anger?'

Then Moorthy feels so desperate that he says to Rachanna's wife, 'And you, Rachanna's wife?' and Rachanna's wife says, 'If my husband says "Spin," I shall spin, learned one.' And Moorthy says he will come back again in the evening, and mopping his forehead, he goes down the steps and along the Pariah street, and going up the promontory, enters the temple, bangs the bell and, performing a circumambulation, asks blessings of the gods, and hurries back home to speak about it all to Rangamma.

But as he goes up the steps something in him says, 'Nay,' and his hair stands on end as he remembers the tumbler of milk and the Pariah home, and so he calls out, 'Rangamma, Rangamma!' and Rangamma says, 'I'm coming,' and when she is at the threshold, he says he has for the first time entered a Pariah house and asks if he is permitted to enter; and Rangamma says, 'Just come the other way round, Moorthy, and there's still hot water in the cauldron and fresh clothes for the meal.' So Moorthy goes by the back yard, and when he has taken his bath and clothed himself, Rangamma says, 'Maybe you'd beter change your holy thread,' but Moorthy says, 'Now that I must go there every day, I cannot change my holy thread every day, can I?' and Rangamma says only, 'I shall at least give you a little Ganges water, and you can take a spoonful of it each time you've touched them, can't you?' So Moorthy says, 'As you will,' and taking the Ganges water he feels a fresher breath flowing through him, and lest anyone should ask about his new adventure, he goes to the riverside after dinner to sit and think and pray. After all a Brahmin is a Brahmin, sister!

And when dusk fell over the river, Moorthy hastily finished his ablutions, and after he had sat at his evening meditations, he rushed back home, and after taking only a banana and a cup of milk, he rushed off again to the Pariah night school that Seenu held in the panchayat hall every evening. And when Seenu heard of the Congress committee to be founded, his mouth touched his ears in joy, and he said he would wake up Kittu and Subbu and Post-office-house Ramu from their inactivity. Moorthy said that would be fine and he went out to see Rachanna who was sitting by the veranda, sharpening his sickle in the moonlight, and with him were Siddanna and Madanna and Lingayya, and when they heard about the Congress committee, they all said, 'As you please, learned master.'—'And your women?' asked Moorthy.—'They will do as we do,' said Rachanna, and Moorthy went again to the Potters' street and the Weavers' street, and they all said, 'If the elder says "Yes," and the patel says "Yes," and the panchayat says "Yes," what else have we to say?' And then he went home and told the whole thing to Rangamma and she too said, 'Of course, of course.' And Seethamma and Ratna said, 'Splendid—a Congress committee here,' and Moorthy said, 'We shall begin work straight off.'

The next morning he went and recounted the whole thing to Range Gowda, and Range Gowda said, 'I am your slave.' Then Moorthy said, 'We shall hold a meeting today'—and Range Gowda said 'Of course,'—'Then this evening,' said Moorthy,— 'As you please, learned one,' answered Range Gowda—and Moorthy then said, 'We shall hold a gods' procession and then a bhajan, and then we shall elect the committee.' And as evening came, Moorthy and Seenu and Ramu and Kittu were all busy washing the gods and knitting the flowers and oiling the wicks and fixing the crowns, and as night fell the procession moved on and people came out with camphor and coconuts, and Seenu took them out and offered them to the gods, and Ramu shouted out "This evening there's bhajan," and everybody was so happy that before the procession was back in the temple, Range Gowda was already seated in the mandap explaining to Elder Ramayya and to Elder Siddayya and to others around them about weaving and ahimsa and the great, great Congress. And they all listened to him with respect. When Moorthy entered they all stood up, but Moorthy said, 'Oh, not this for me!' and Range

Gowda said, 'You are our Gandhi,' and when everybody laughed he went on: 'There is nothing to laugh at, brothers. He is our Gandhi. The state of Mysore has a maharaja, but that maharaja has another maharaja who is in London, and that one has another one in heaven, and so everybody has his own Mahatma, and this Moorthy, who has been caught in our knees playing as a child, is now grown up and great, and he has wisdom in him and he will be our Mahatma,' and they all said, 'So he is!' And Moorthy felt such a quiet exaltation rise to his throat that a tear escaped and ran down his cheek. Then he looked back toward the bright god in the sanctum, and closed his eyes and sent up a prayer, and, whispering to himself, '*Mahatma Gandhi ki jai*,' he rang the bell and spoke to them of spinning and ahimsa and truth. And then he asked, 'who among you will join the panchayat?' and voices came from the Sudra corner and the Pariah corner and the Brahmin corner and the Weavers' corner, and to each one of them he said, 'Stand before the god and vow you will never break the law,' and some said they asked nothing of the gods, and others said, 'We don't know whether we have the strength to keep it up,' and then Range Gowda grew wild and shouted, 'If you are the sons of your fathers, stand up and do what this learned boy says,' and Range Gowda's words were such a terror to them that one here and one there went up before the sanctum, rang the bell and said, 'My master, I shall spin a hundred yards of yarn per day, and I shall practise ahimsa, and I shall seek truth,' and they fell prostrate and asked for the blessings of the Mahatma and the gods, and they rose and crawled back to their seats. But when it comes to the Pariahas, Rachanna says, 'We shall stand out here and take the vows,' and at this Moorthy is so confused that he does not know what to do, but Range Gowda says, 'Here in the temple or there in the courtyard, it is the same god you vow before, so go along!' And Rachanna and Rachanna's wife, and Madanna and Madanna's wife swear before the god from the courtyard steps.

And when it is all over, Range Gowda says, 'Moorthappa will be our president,' and everybody says, 'Of course, of course.' Then Seenu turns towards Range Gowda and says, 'And Range Gowda our super-president and protector,' and everybody laughs, and Range Gowda says, 'Protector! yes, protector of the village fowl!' Then Seenu says, 'Rangamma will be the third member,' but Rangamma says, 'No, no,' and Moorthy says, 'We need a woman in the committee for the Congress is for the weak and the lowly'; and then everybody says, 'Rangamma, say yes!' and Rangamma says, 'Yes.' And Moorthy then turns toward the Pariaha and says, 'One among you!' and then there is such a silence that a moving ant could be heard, and then Moorthy says, 'Come, Rachanna, you have suffered much, and you shall be a member,' and Rachanna says, 'As you will, learned master!' And then Moorthy says, 'Seenu is our fifth member,' and Range Gowda says, 'Every Rama needs an Anjanayya, and he's your fire-tailed Hanuman,' and they all laugh, and so Moorthy and Range Gowda and Rangamma and Rachanna and Seenu become the Congress panchayat committee of Kanthapura.

And two days later Moorthy made a list of members and twenty-three were named, and five rupees and twelve annas were sent to the provisional Congress committee. And one morning everybody was told that in Rangamma's blue paper was a picture of Moorthy. And everybody went to Rangamma and said, 'Show it to me!' and when Ranagmma gave them the paper, they looked this side and that, and when they came to the picture, they all exlaimed. 'Oh, here he is—and so much like him too!' And then they all said, 'Our Moorthy is a great man, and they speak of him in the city and we shall work for him,' and from then onward we all began to spin more and more, and more and more, and Moorthy sent bundles and bundles of yarn, and we got saris and bodice cloths and dhotis, and Moorthy said the Mahatma was very pleased. Maybe he would remember us!

(From *Kanthapura*, New Directions, New York, 1963)

The Cow of the Barricades

Gauri, fashioning waters, has lived and measured out, she the one-footed, two-footed, four-footed, eight-footed, and also becoming nine-footed. She is the Thousand-Syllabled in the highest heaven.

—RIG VEDA

THEY called her Gauri, for she came every Tuesday evening before sunset to stand and nibble at the hair of the Master. And the Master touched her and caressed her and he said: 'How are you, Gauri?' and Gauri simply bent her legs and drew back her tongue and, shaking her head, ambled round him and disappeared among the bushes. And till Tuesday next she was not to be seen. And the Master's disciples gathered grain and grass and rice-water to give her every Tuesday, but she refused it all and took only the handful of grain the Master gave. She munched it slowly and carefully as one articulates a string of holy words, and when she had finished eating, she knelt again, shook her head and disappeared. And the Master's disciples said, 'This is a strange creature,' and they went to the Cotton Street and the Mango Street, and they went by the Ginning Mills and through the Weavers' Lines, but Gauri was nowhere to be seen. She was not even a god-dedicated cow, for never had a shopkeeper caught her eating the grams nor was she found huddled in a cattle-pound. People said, 'Only the Master could have such strange visitors,' and they went to the Master and said: 'Master, can you tell us who this cow may be?' And the Master smiled with unquenchable love and fun and he said: 'She may be my baton-armed mother-in-law. Though she may be the mother of any one of you. Perhaps she is the great Mother's vehicle.' And like to a mother, they put kumkum on her forehead, and till Tuesday next they waited for Gauri.

But people heard of it here and people heard of it there, and they came with grain and hay and kumkum water saying, 'We have a strange visitor, let us honour her.' And merchants came saying, 'Maybe she's Lakshmi, the Goddess, and we may make more money next harvest,' and fell at her feet. And students came to touch her head and touch her tail, saying, 'Let me pass the examinations this year!' And young girls came to ask for husbands and widows to ask for purity, and the childless to ask for children. And so every Tuesday there was a veritable procession of people at the Master's hermitage. But Gauri would pass by them all like a holy wife among men, and going straight to the Master, would nibble at his hair and disappear among the bushes. People unable to take back the untouched offerings gave them to the river and the fishes jumped to eat them as at a festival; but the crocodile had disappeared from the whirls of the deep waters. And one fine morning the Master woke in his bed to hear the snake and the rat playing under him, for when the seeker finds harmony, the jackal and the deer and the rat and the serpent become friends. And Gauri was no doubt a fervent soul who had sought the paths of this world to be born a sage in the next, for she was so compassionate and true.

There was only one other person whose hair she had nibbled —she had nibbled at the hair of Mahatma Gandhi. For the Mahatma loved all creatures, the speechful and mute.

Now at this time the Mahatma's men were fighting in the country against the red-men's Government. The Mahatma said: 'Don't buy their cloth.' And people did not buy their cloth. The Mahatma said: 'Don't serve under them.' And people did not serve under them. And the Mahatma said: 'Don't pay their taxes.' And people gathered, and bonfires were lit and processions were formed, and there were many men wounded and killed and many taken to prisons, but people would not pay taxes nor would they wear foreign clothes. And soldiers came from the cities, big men, and bearded men, with large rifles and they said to some, 'You shall not leave the house after, sunset'; and to some, 'You shall not ride a bicycle'; and to yet others, 'You shall not go out of the district.' And children carried blue cards when they were good, blue and red when they were a little wicked, and red when they were very wicked. And women could not go to the temples and marriages, and men could not go to the riverside to ease themselves in the morning. Life became intolerable and people moaned and groaned, but the red-men's Government would rule the country, happen what may, and make men pay more and more taxes.

Then the men in the mills and factories said, 'We are with you, brothers,' and the women said, 'We are with you, sisters,' and the whole town became a battle-ground. For, when the soldiers had passed through the streets, the workers of the mills builded barricade after barricade. With stones and bamboos and bedsteads and carts and mill-stones and granary-baskets they builded barricades, and the soldiers could not pass again. The Master came and said: 'No barricades in the name of the Mahatma, for much blood will be spilt,' but the workmen said, 'It is not with, "I love you, I love you," you can change the grinding heart of this Government.' And they built more and more barricades and put themselves behind these, and one day they were the masters of the town.

But the red-men's Government was no fool's government. It sent for men from Peshawar and Pindi, while heavy cars were stationed at the City Gates, with guns to the left and guns to the right, and soldiers stood beside them, for the town would be taken and cost what it might the red-men's Government would govern.

And, though Gauri had neither the blue card nor the red card she now came every evening to the Master; she looked very sad, and somebody had even seen a tear, clear as a drop of the Ganges, run down her cheeks, for she was of compassion infinite and true.

And people were much affrighted, and they took the women and the children to the fields beyond and they cooked food beneath the trees and lived there—for the army of the Government was going to take the town and no woman or child would be spared. And doors were closed and clothes and vessels and jewels were hidden away, and only the workmen and the men ruled the city, and the Master was the head of them all, and they called him President. Patrols of young men in khadi and Gandhi-cap would go through the streets, and when they saw the old or the miserly peeping from behind the doors they called them and talked to them and led them to the camp by the fields, for the Master said there was danger and nobody could stay but the strong and the young. Grass grew beneath the eaves and dust of monsoon swept along the streets while the red-men's trains brought armies after armies, and everybody could see them, for the station was down below and the town upon a hill. Barricades lay on the streets like corpse-heaps after the last plague, but the biggest of them all was in the Suryanarayana Street. It was as big as a chariot.

Men were hid behind it and waited for the battle. But the Master said, 'No, there shall be no battle, brothers.' But the workmen said again, 'It is not with, "I love you, I love you," that you can change the grinding heart of this Government,' and they brought picks and scythes and crowbars, and a few Mohammedans brought their swords and one or two stole rifles from the mansions, and there was a regular fighting army ready to fall on the red-man's men. And the Master went and said this and the Master went and said that, but the workmen said,

'We'll fight,' and fight they would. So deep in despair the Master said, 'I resign from the Presidentship,' and he went and sat in meditation and rose into the worlds from which come light and love, in order that the city might be saved from bloodshed. And when people heard this they were greatly angered against the workmen, but they knew the workmen were right and the Master was right, and they did not know which way the eye should turn. Owls hovered about even in midday light, and when dusk fell, all the stars hung so low that people knew that that night would see the fight.

But everybody looked at the empty street-corners and said, 'Where is she—Gauri?'

At ten that night the first war-chariots were heard to move up, and cannons and bayonets and lifted swords rushed in assault.

And what happened afterwards people remember to this very day. There she was, Gauri, striding out of the Oil Lane and turning round Copper Seenayya's house towards the Suryanarayana Street, her head held gently bent and her ears pressed back like plaits of hair, and staggering like one going to the temple with fruits and flowers to offer to the Goddess. And she walked fast, fast, and when people saw her they ran behind her, and crowds after crowds gathered round her, and torch and lantern in hand they marched through the Brahmin Street and the Cotton Street and past the Venkatalakshamma Well, and the nearer she came to the barricades the faster she walked, though she never ran. And people said, 'She will protect us. Now it's sure she will save us,' and bells were brought and rung and camphors were lit and coconuts were broken at her feet, but she neither shuddered nor did she move her head; she walked on. And the workmen who were behind the barricades, they saw this and they were sore furious with it, and they said, 'Here, they send the cow instead of coming to help us.' Some swore and others laughed, and one of them said, 'We'll fire at her, for if the crowd is here and the red-men's army on the other side, it will be terrible.' But they were afraid, for the crowd chanted 'Vande Mataram,' and they were all uplifted and sure, and Gauri marched onwards her eyes raised towards the barricades. And as she came near the Temple-square the workmen lay down their arms, as she came by the Tulasi Well they folded their hands, and as she was beneath the barricades they fell prostrate at her feet murmuring, 'Goddess, who may you be?' And they formed two rings, and between them passed Gauri, her left foreleg first, then her back right leg, once on the sand-bag, once on the cart-wheel, and with the third move men pushed her up and she was on the top of the barricades. And then came a rich whispering like a crowd at evening worship, but the red-men's army cried from the other side of the barricades, 'Oh, what's this? Oh, what's this?' and they rushed towards the barricades thinking it was a flag of truce. But when they saw the cow and its looks and the tear, clear as a drop of the Ganges, they shouted out, 'Victory to the Mahatma! Mahatma Gandhi ki jai!' and joined up with the crowd. But their chief, the red-man, saw this and fired a shot. It went through Gauri's head, and she fell, a vehicle of God among lowly men.

But they said blood did not gush out of the head but only between the forelegs, from the thickness of her breast.

Peace has come back to us now. Seth Jamnalal Dwarak Chand bought the two houses on either side of the barricades, cut a loop road through them, and in the middle he erected a metal statue for Gauri. Our Gauri was not so tall nor was she so stiff, for she had a very human look. But we all offer her flowers and honey and perfumed sweetmeats and the first green grass of spring. And our children jump over the railings and play between her legs, and putting their mouths to the hole in the breast —for this was made too—shout out resounding booms. And never have our carpenters had gayer times than since Gauri died, for our children do not want their baswanna-bulls but only ask for Gauris. And to this day hawkers cry them about at the railway station, chanting, 'Gauris of Gorakhpur! Polished, varnished and on four wheels!' and many a child from the far Himalayas to the seas of the South pulls them through the dusty streets of Hindusthan.

But even now when we light our sanctum lights at night, we say, 'Where is she, Gauri?' Only the Master knows where she is. He says: 'Gauri is waiting in the Middle Heavens to be born. She will be reborn when India sorrows again before She is free.'

Therefore it is said, 'The Mahatma may be all wrong about politics, but he is right about the fullness of love in all creatures —the speechful and the mute.'

(From *The Policeman and the Rose*, Oxford University Press, New Delhi).

8. KHUSHWANT SINGH

Khushwant Singh was born in 1915 at Hadali, Punjab (now in Pakistan). He was educated at a public school in Lahore and later at St Stephen's College, Delhi. He went to England for higher education and joined King's College, London. He was also called to the bar. After a stint at the Law Courts in Lahore, he served as a Press Attache in the Indian High Commission at London and at Toronto. In 1950 he published *The Mark of Vishnu and other Stories* which brought him into prominence as a story writer. But his major work is *Mano Majra* (1956), better known by its alternate title *Train to Pakistan*, for which he was awarded the Grove press fiction prize. He has so far published four collections of short stories and two novels, besides a two-volume history of the Sikhs and Sikhism, *A History of the Sikhs* (1963-1966). He has lectured on comparative religion and law at several American colleges and universites.

His writings are characterized by a sense of realism and humour, and his use of English in his novels is distinctive in that he employs his native Punjabi expressions and conversational idiom. His style, though occasionally pedestrian, is notable for its verve, comic spirit and gaiety.

Train to Pakistan (1956) is as much a social document as it is a work of literary art. Like Manohar Malgonkar's *A Bend in the Ganges*, it is based on a historic event, the partition of India into two independent states resulting in genocide and migration of millions from one state to the other.

The time is 1947. A little village, Mano Majra, close to the Indo-Pakistan border, provides the setting for the novel. It is a village where Hindus and Muslims have for centuries lived together in peace. But even this tiny village is engulfed by the bitter and bloody communal conflict generated by the partition.

Malli, a dacoit, murders Ram Lal, a village moneylender, and carries away his gold. He throws bangles into the house of Jagat Singh (Jugga), a notorious 'tough' of the village, as a mark of insult and challenge. Jugga at that time is away in the fields making love to Nooran, daughter of a Muslim weaver. When he returns to the village, he finds the people gravely agitated over the dacoity and murder. Hukum Chand, the Divisional Magistrate, has at this very time been dallying with Haseena, a young prostitute, but on hearing the gun-shots he swears and hurriedly leaves the place.

Policemen arrive at Mano Majra the next day to inquire into Ram Lal's murder. Iqbal Singh, a westernized youth, also arrives to work for a socialistic revolution in the countryside. He is by mistake arrested by the police, although he is liked by the Sikh priest, Meet Singh, and the village Lambardar. His very name is ambiguous, as it could mean a Hindu, a Muslim, or a Sikh.

Mano Majra is in the grip of panic and fear accentuated by the arrival of a train from Pakistan filled with corpses. The Sikhs, Muslims and Hindus, who have been living there in harmony, become suspicious of each other. The gruesome tales of the refugees from Pakistan incense the Hindu fanatics, who vow to take revenge. The Muslims are to be evacuated to a camp at Chandannagar. Before their evacuation they meet their Hindu and Sikh friends in the village and bid them a touching farewell. Nooran, who is with Jugga's child, visits Jugga's mother to bid her goodbye before moving to the refugee camp from where the Muslims are to travel by train to Pakistan. Hukum Chand's Haseena is also to be on the same train to Pakistan. Hukum Chand releases Jugga on purpose. Jugga comes to know of the plot hatched by the Hindu and Sikh fanatics to blow up the train as it crosses the bridge on its way to Pakistan. In utter disregard of his own safety, Jugga climbs up the steel spans of the bridge and starts slashing at the ropes connecting the dynamite to the bridge. The leader of the saboteurs fires at him, but Jugga, though wounded, clings to the rope with his hand and manages to cut it, although in the process he falls down and is run over by the train.

The novel, thus, also dramatizes a lover's supreme sacrifice to save his beloved.

What follows is the third section in the novel (Grove Press edition), when a train filled with corpses arrives from Pakistan:

Train to Pakistan

When it was discovered that the train had brought a full load of corpses, a heavy brooding silence descended on the village. People barricaded their doors and many stayed up all night talking in whispers. Everyone felt his neighbor's hand against him, and thought of finding friends and allies. They did not notice the clouds blot out the stars nor smell the cool damp breeze. When they woke up in the morning and saw it was raining, their first thoughts were about the train and the burning corpses. The whole village was on the roofs looking toward the station.

The train had disappeared as mysteriously as it had come. The station was deserted. The soldier's tents were soaked with water and looked depressing. There was no smoldering fire nor smoke. In fact there was no sign of life—or death. Still people watched; perhaps there would be another train with more corpses!

By afternoon the clouds had rolled away to the west. Rain had cleared the atmosphere and one could see for miles around. Villagers ventured forth from their homes to find out if anyone knew more than they. Then they went back to their roofs. Although it had stopped raining, no one could be seen on the station platform or in the passenger shed or the military camp. A row of vultures sat on the parapet of the station building and kites were flying in circles high above it.

The head constable, with his posse of policemen and prisoners, was spotted a long way away from the village. People shouted the information to each other. The lambardar was summoned. When the head constable arrived with his party, there was quite a crowd assembled under the peepul tree near the temple.

The head constable unlocked the handcuffs of the prisoners in front of the villagers. They were made to put their thumb impressions on pieces of paper and told to report to the police station twice a week. The villagers looked on sullenly. They knew that Jugga budmash and the stranger had nothing to do with the dacoity. They were equally certain that in arresting Malli's gang the police were on the right track. Perhaps they were not all involved; some of the five might have been arrested mistakenly. It was scarcely possible that none of them had had anything to do with it. Yet there were the police letting them loose—not in their own village, but in Mano Majra where they had committed the murder. The police must be certain of their innocence to take such a risk.

The head constable took the lambardar aside and the two spoke to each other for sometime. The lambardar came back and addressed the villagers saying: 'The Sentry Sahib wants to know if anyone here has seen or heard anything about Sultana budmash or any of his gang.'

Several villagers came out with news. He was known to have gone away to Pakistan along with his gang. They were all Muslims, and Muslims of their village had been evacuated.

'Was it before or after the murder of the Lala that he left?' inquired the head constable, coming up beside the lambardar.

'After,' they answered in a chorus. There was a long pause. The villagers looked at each other somewhat puzzled. Was it them? Before they could ask the policemen any questions, the head constable was speaking again.

"Did any of you see or talk to a young Mussulman babu called Mohammed Iqbal who was a member of the Muslim League?'

The lambardar was taken aback. He did not know Iqbal was a Muslim. He vaguely recalled Meet Singh and Imam Baksh calling him Iqbal Singh. He looked in the crowd for Imam Baksh but could not find him. Several villagers started telling the head constable excitedly of having seen Iqbal go to the fields and loiter about the railway track near the bridge.

'Did you notice anything suspicious about him?'

'Suspicious? Well...'

'Did you notice anything suspicious about the fellow?'

'Did you?'

No one was sure. One could never be sure about educated people; they were all suspiciously cunning. Surely Meet Singh was the one to answer questions about the babu; some of the babu's things were still with him in the gurdwara.

Meet Singh was pushed up to the front.

The head constable ignored Meet Singh and again addressed the group who had been answering him. 'I will speak to the bhai later,' he said. 'Can any one of you say whether this man came to Mano Majra before or after the dacoity?'

This was another shock. What would an urban babu have to do with dacoity or murder? Maybe it was not for money after all! No one was quite sure. Now they were not sure of anything. The head constable dismissed the meeting with: 'If anyone has any authentic information about the moneylender's murder or about Sultana or about Mohammed Iqbal, report at the police station at once.'

The crowd broke into small groups, talking and gesticulating animatedly. Meet Singh went up to the head constable who was getting his constables ready to march back.

'Sentry Sahib, the young man you arrested the other day is not a Mussulman. He is a Sikh—Iqbal Singh.'

The head constable took no notice of him. He was busy writing something on a piece of yellow paper. Meet Singh waited patiently.

'Sentry Sahib,' he started again as the other was folding the paper. The head constable did not even look at him. He beckoned one of the constables and handed him the paper saying:

Get a bicycle or a tonga and take this letter to the commandant of the Pakistan military unit. Also tell him yourself that you have come from Mano Majra and the situation is serious. He must send his trucks and soldiers to evacuate the Muslims as early as possible. At once.'

'Yes, sir,' answered the constable clicking his heels.

'Sentry Sahib,' implored Meet Singh.

'Sentry Sahib, Sentry Sahib, Sentry Sahib,' repeated the head constable angrily. 'You have been eating my ears with your 'Sentry Sahibs. What do you want?'

'Iqbal Singh is a Sikh.'

'Did you open the fly-buttons of his pants to see whether he was a Sikh or a Mussulman? You are a simple bhai of a temple. Go and pray.'

The head constable took his place in front of the policemen standing in double file.

'Attention! By the left, quick march.'

Meet Singh turned back to the temple without answering the eager queries of the villagers.

The head constable's visit had divided Mano Majra into two halves as neatly as a knife cuts through a pat of butter.

Muslims sat and moped in their houses. Rumors of atrocities committed by Sikhs on Muslims in Patiala, Ambala and Kapurthala, which they had heard and dismissed, came back to their minds. They had heard of gentlewomen having their veils taken off, being stripped and marched down crowded streets to be raped in the market place. Many had eluded their would-be ravishers by killing themselves. They had heard of mosques being desecrated by the slaughter of pigs on the premises, and of copies of the holy Koran being torn up by infidels. Quite suddenly every Sikh in Mano Majra became a stranger with an evil intent. His long hair and beard appeared barbarous, his kirpan menacingly anti-Muslim. For the first time, the name Pakistan came to mean something to them—a haven of refuge where there were no Sikhs.

The Sikhs were sullen and angry. 'Never trust a Mussulman,' they said. The last Guru had warned them that Muslims had no loyalties. He was right. All through the Muslim period of Indian history, sons had imprisoned or killed their own fathers and brothers had blinded brothers to get the throne. And what had they done to the Sikhs? Executed two of their Gurus, assassinated another and butchered his infant children; hundreds of thousands had been put to the sword for no other offense than refusing to accept Islam; their temples had been desecrated by the slaughter of kine; the holy Granth had been torn to bits. And Muslims were never ones to respect women. Sikh refugees had told of women jumping into wells and burning themselves rather than fall into the hands of Muslims. Those who did not commit suicide were paraded naked in the streets, raped in public, and then murdered. Now a trainload of Sikhs massacred by Muslims had been cremated in Mano Majra. Hindus and Sikhs were fleeing from their homes in Pakistan and having to find shelter in Mano Majra. Then there was the murder of Ram Lal. No one knew who had killed him, but everyone knew Ram Lal was a Hindu; Sultana and his gang were Muslims and had fled to Pakistan. An unknown character—without turban or beard— had been loitering about the village. These were reasons enough to be angry with someone. So they decided to be angry with the Muslims; Muslims were basely ungrateful. Logic was never a strong point with Sikhs; when they were roused, logic did not matter at all.

It was a gloomy night. The breeze that had swept away the clouds blew them back again. At first they came in fleecy strands of white. The moon wiped them off its face. Then they came in large billows, blotted out the moonlight and turned the sky a dull gray. The moon fought its way through and occasionally patches of the plain sparkled like silver. Later, clouds came in monstrous black formations and spread across the sky. Then without any lightning or thunder it began to rain.

A group of Sikh peasants gathered together in the house of the lambardar. They sat in a circle around a hurricane lantern—some on a charpoy, others on the floor. Meet Singh was amongst them.

For a long time nobody said anything apart from repeating, 'God is punishing us for our sins.'

'Yes, God is punishing us for our sins.'

'There is a lot of *zulum* in Pakistan.'

'That is because He wants to punish us for our sins. Bad acts yield a bitter harvest.'

Then one of the younger men spoke. 'What have we done to deserve this? We have looked upon the Muslims as our brothers and sisters. Why should they send somebody to spy on us?'

'You mean Iqbal?' Meet Singh said. 'I had quite a long conversation with him. He had an iron bangle on his wrist like all of us Sikhs and told me that his mother had wanted him to wear it, so he wore it. He is a shaven Sikh. He does not smoke. And he came the day after the moneylender's murder.'

'Bhai you get taken in easily,' replied the same youth. 'Does it hurt a Mussulman to wear an iron bangle or not smoke for a day—particularly if he has some important work to do?'

'I may be a simple bhai,' protested Meet Singh warmly, 'but I know as well as you that the babu had nothing to do with the murder; he would not have been in the village afterwards if he had. That any fathead would understand.'

The youth felt a little abashed.

'Besides that,' continued Meet Singh more confidently, 'they had already arrested Malli for the dacoity...'

'How do you know what they had arrested Malli for?' interrupted the youth triumphantly.

'Yes, how do you know what the police know? They have released Malli. Have you ever known them to release murderers without a trial and acquittal?' asked some others.

'Bhai, you always talk without reason.'

'Accha, if you are the ones with all the reason, tell me who threw the packet of bangles into Jugga's house?'

'How should we know?' answered a chorus.

'I will tell you. It was Jugga's enemy Malli. You all know they had fallen out. Who else would dare insult Jugga except he?'

No one answered the question. Meet Singh went on aggressively to drive his point home. 'And all this about Sultana, Sultana! What has that to do with the dacoity?'

'Yes, Bhaiji, you may be right,' said another youth. 'But Lala is dead: why bother about him? The police will do that. Let Jugga, Malli and Sultana settle their quarrels. As for the babu, for all we care he can sleep with his mother. Our problem is: what are we to do with all these pigs we have with us? They have been eating our salt for generations and see what they have done! We have treated them like our own brothers. They have behaved like snakes.'

The temperature of the meeting went up suddenly. Meet Singh spoke angrily.

'What have they done to you? Have they ousted you from your lands or occupied your houses? Have they seduced your womenfolk? Tell me, what have they done?'

'Ask the refugees what they have done to them,' answered the truculent youth who had started the argument. 'You mean to tell us that they are lying when they say that gurdwaras have been burned and people massacred?'

'I was only talking of Mano Majra. What have our tenants done?'

'They are Muslims.'

Meet Singh shrugged his shoulders.

The lambardar felt it was up to him to settle the argument.

'What had to happen has happened,' he said wisely. 'We have to decide what we are to do now. These refugees who have turned up at the temple may do something which will bring a bad name on the village.'

The reference to 'something' changed the mood of the meeting. How could outsiders dare do "something" to their fellow villagers? Here was another stumbling block to logic. Group loyalty was above reason. The youth who had referred to Muslims as pigs spoke haughtily: 'We would like to see somebody raise his little finger against our tenants while we live!'

The lambardar snubbed him. 'You are a hotheaded one. Sometimes you want to kill Muslims. Sometimes you want to kill refugees. We say something and you drag the talk to something else.'

'All right, all right, Lambardara,' retorted the young man, 'if you are all that clever, you say something.'

'Listen, brothers,' said the lambardar lowering his voice. 'This is no time to lose tempers. Nobody here wants to kill anyone. But who knows the intentions of other people? Today we have forty or fifty refugees, who by the grace of the Guru are a peaceful lot and they only talk. Tomorrow we may get others who may have lost their mothers or sisters. Are we going to tell them: 'do not come to this village?' And if they do come, will we let them wreak vengeance on our tenants?'

'You have said something worth a hundred thousand rupees,' said an old man. 'We should think about it.'

The peasants thought about their problem. They could not refuse shelter to refugees: hospitality was not a pastime but a sacred duty when those who sought it were homeless. Could they ask their Muslims to go? Quite emphatically not! Loyalty to a fellow villager was above all other considerations. Despite the words they had used, no one had the nerve to suggest throwing them out, even in a purely Sikh gathering. The mood of the assembly changed from anger to bewilderment.

After some time the lambardar spoke.

'All Muslims of the neighbouring villages have been evacuated and taken to the refugee camp near Chundunnugger. Some have already gone away to Pakistan. Others have been sent to the bigger camp at Jullundur.'

'Yes,' added another. 'Kapoora and Gujjoo Matta were evacuated last week. Mano Majra is the only place left where there are Muslims. What I would like to know is how these people asked their fellow villagers to leave. We could never say anything like that to our tenants, any more than we could tell our sons to get out of our homes. Is there anyone here who could say to the Muslims, 'Brothers, you should go away from Mano Majra?'

Before anyone could answer another villager came in and stood on the threshold. Everyone turned round to see, but they could not recognize him in the dim lamplight.

'Who is it?' asked the lambardar, shading his eyes from the lamp. 'Come in.'

Imam Baksh came in. Two others followed him. They also were Muslims.

'Salaam, Chacha Imam Baksh, Salaam Khair Dina. Salaam, salaam.'

'Sat Sri Akal, Lambardara. Sat Sri Akal.' answered the Muslims.

People made room for them and waited for Imam Baksh to begin.

Imam Baksh combed his beard with his fingers.

'Well, brothers, what is your decision about us?' he asked quietly.

There was an awkward silence. Everyone looked at the lambardar.

'Why ask us?' answered the lambardar. 'This is your village as much as ours.'

'You have heard what is being said! All the neighbouring villages have been evacuated. Only we are left. If you want us to go too, we will go.'

Meet Singh began to sniff. He felt it was not for him to speak.

He had said his bit. Besides, he was only a priest who lived on what the villagers gave him. One of the younger men spoke.

'It is like this, Uncle Imam Baksh. As long as we are here nobody will dare to touch you. We die first and then you can look after yourselves.'

'Yes,' added another warmly, 'we first, then you. If anyone raises his eyebrows at you will rape his mother.'

'Mother, sister and daughter,' added the others.

Imam Baksh wiped a tear from his eyes and blew his nose in the hem of his shirt.

'What have we to do with Pakistan? We were born here. So were our ancestors. We have lived amongst you as brothers.' Imam Baksh broke down. Meet Singh clasped him in his arms and began to sob. Several of the people started crying quietly and blowing their noses.

The lambardar spoke: 'Yes, you are our brothers. As far as we are concerned, you and your children and your grandchildren can live here as long as you like. If anyone speaks rudely to you, your wives or your children, it will be us first and our wives and children before a single hair of your heads is touched. But Chacha, we are so few and the strangers coming from Pakistan are coming in thousands. Who will be responsible for what they do?'

'Yes,' agreed the others, 'as far as we are concerned you are all right, but what about these refugees?'

'I have heard that some villages were surrounded by mobs many thousands strong, all armed with guns and spears. There was no question of resistance.'

'We are not afraid of mobs,' replied another quicky. 'Let them come! We will give them such a beating they will not dare to look at Mano Majra again.'

Nobody took notice of the challenger; the boast sounded too hollow to be taken seriously. Imam Baksh blew his nose again.

'What do you advise us to do then, brothers?' he asked,

choking with emotion.

'Uncle,' said the lambardar in a heavy voice, 'it is very hard for me to say, but seeing the sort of time we live in, I would advise you to go to the refugee camp while this trouble is on. You lock your houses with your belongings. We will look after your cattle till you come back.'

The lambardar's advice created a tense stillness. Villagers held their breath for fear of being heard. The lambardar himself felt that he ought to say something quickly to dispel the effect of his words.

'Until yesterday,' he began again loudly, 'in case of trouble we could have helped you to cross the river by the ford. Now it has been raining for two days; the river has risen. The only crossings are by trains and road bridges—you know what is happening there! It is for your own safety that I advise you to take shelter in the camp for a few days, and then you can come back. As far as we are concerned,' he repeated warmly, 'if you decide to stay on, you are most welcome to do so. We will defend you with our lives.'

No one had any doubts about the import of the lambardar's words. They sat with their heads bowed till Imam Baksh stood up.

'All right, he said solemnly, 'if we have to go, we better pack up our bedding and belongings. It will take us more than one night to clear out of homes it has taken our fathers and grandfathers hundreds of years to make.'

The lambardar felt a strong sense of guilt and was overcome with emotion. He got up and embraced Imam Baksh and started to cry loudly. Sikh and Muslim villagers fell into each other's arms and wept like children. Imam Baksh gently got out of the lambardar's embrace. 'There is no need to cry.' he said between sobs. 'This is the way of the world—

Not forever does the bulbul sing

*In balmy shades of bowers,
Not forever lasts the spring
Nor ever blossom flowers.
Not forever reigneth joy,*

*Sets the sun on days of bliss,
Friendships not forever last,
They know not life, who know not this.*

'They know not life, who know not this,' repeated many others with sighs. 'Yes, Uncle Imam Baksh. This is life.'

Imam Baksh and his companions left the meeting in tears.

Before going round to other Muslim homes, Imam Baksh went to his own hut attached to the mosque. Nooran was already in bed. An oil lamp burned in a niche in the wall.

'Nooro, Nooro,' he shouted, shaking her by the shoulder. 'Get up, Nooro.'

The girl opened her eyes. 'What is the matter?'

'Get up and pack. We have to go away tomorrow morning,' he announced dramatically.

'Go away? Where?'

'I don't know.. .Pakistan!'

The girl sat up with a jerk. 'I will not go to Pakistan,' she said defiantly.

Imam Baksh pretended he had not heard. 'Put all the clothes in the trunks and the cooking utensils in a gunny bag. Also take something for the buffalo. We will have to take her too.'

'I will not go to Pakistan,' the girl repeated fiercely.

'You may not want to go, but they will throw you out. All Muslims are leaving for the camp tomorrow.'

'Who will throw us out? This is our village. Are the police and the government dead?'

'Don't be silly, girl. Do as you are told. Hundreds of thousands of people are going to Pakistan and as many coming out.

Those who stay behind are killed. Hurry up and pack. I have to go and tell the others that they must get ready.'

Imam Baksh left the girl sitting up in bed. Nooran rubbed her face with her hands and stared at the wall. She did not know what to do. She could spend the night out and come back when all the others had gone. But she could not do it alone; and it was raining. Her only chance was Jugga. Malli had been released, maybe Jugga had also come home. She knew that was not true, but the hope persisted and it gave her something to do.

Nooran went out in the rain. She passed many people in the lanes, going about with gunny bags covering their heads and shoulders. The whole village was awake. In most houses she could see the dim flickers of oil lamps. Some were packing; others were helping them to pack. Most just talked with their friends. The women sat on the floors hugging each other and crying. It was as if in every home there had been a death.

Nooran shook the door of Jugga's house. The chain on the other side rattled but there was no response. In the gray light she noticed the door was bolted from the outside. She undid the iron ring and went in. Jugga's mother was out, probably visiting some Muslim friends. There was no light at all. Nooran sat down on a charpoy. She did not want to face Jugga's mother alone nor did she want to go back home. She hoped something would happen—something which would make Jugga walk in. She sat and waited and hoped.

For an hour Nooran watched the gray shadows of clouds chasing each other. It drizzled and poured and poured and drizzled alternately. She heard the sound of footsteps cautiously picking their way through the muddy lane. They stopped outside the door. Someone shook the door.

'Who is it?' asked an old woman's voice.

Nooran lost her nerve; she did not move.

'Who is it?' demanded the voice angrily. 'Why don't you speak?'

Nooran stood up and mumbled indistinctly, 'Beybey.'

The old woman stepped in and quickly shut the door behind her.

'Jugga! Jugga, is it you?' she whispered. 'Have they let you off?'

'No, Beybey, it is I—Nooran. Chacha Imam Baksh's daughter,' answered the girl timidly.

'Nooro? What brings you here at this hour?' the old woman asked angrily?

'Has Jugga come back?'

'What have you to do with Jugga?' his mother snapped. 'You have sent him to jail. You have made him a budmash. Does your father know you go about to strangers' houses at midnight like a tart?'

Nooran began to cry. 'We are going away tomorrow.'

That did not soften the old woman's heart.

'What relation are you to us that you want to come to see us? You can go where you like.'

Nooran played her last card. 'I cannot leave. Jugga has promised to marry me.'

'Get out, you bitch!' the old woman hissed. 'You, a Muslim weaver's daughter, marry a Sikh peasant! Get out, or I will go and tell your father and the whole village. Go to Pakistan! Leave my Jugga alone.'

Nooran felt heavy and lifeless. 'All right, Beybey, I will go. Don't be angry with me. When Jugga comes back just tell him I came to say "Sat Sri Akal".' The girl went down on her knees, clasped the old woman's legs and began to sob. 'Beybey, I am going away and will never come back again. Don't be harsh to me just when I am leaving.'

Jugga's mother stood stiff, without a trace of emotion on her face. Inside her, she felt a little weak and soft. 'I will tell Jugga.'

Nooran stopped crying. Her sobs came at long intervals. She still held onto Jugga's mother. Her head sank lower and lower till it touched the old woman's feet.

'Beybey.'

'What have you to say now?' She had a premonition of what was coming.

'Beybey.'

'Beybey! Beybey! Why don't you say something?' asked the woman, pushing Nooran away. 'What is it?'

The girl swallowed the spittle in her mouth.

'Beybey, I have Jugga's child inside me. If I go to Pakistan they will kill it when they know it has a Sikh father.'

The old woman let Nooran's head drop back on her feet. Nooran clutched them hard and began to cry again.

'How long have you had it?'

'I have just found out. It is the second month.'

Jugga's mother helped Nooran up and the two sat down on the charpoy. Nooran stopped sobbing.

'I cannot keep you here,' said the old woman at last. 'I have enough trouble with the police already. When all this is over and Jugga comes back, he will go and get you from wherever you are. Does your father know?'

'No! If he finds out he will marry me off to someone or murder me.' She started crying again.

'Oh, stop this whining,' commanded the old woman sternly. 'Why didn't you think of it when you were at the mischief? I have already told you Jugga will get you as soon as he is out.'

Nooran stifled her sobs.

'Beybey, don't let him be too long.'

'He will hurry for his own sake. If he does not get you he will have to buy a wife and there is not a pice or trinket left with us. He will get you if he wants a wife. Have no fear.'

A vague hope filled Nooran's being. She felt as if she belonged to the house and the house to her; the charpoy she sat on, the buffalo, Jugga's mother, all were hers. She could come back even if Jugga failed to turn up. She could tell them she was married.

The thought of her father came like a dark cloud over her lunar hopes. She would slip away without telling him. The moon shone again.

'Beybey, if I get the chance I will come to say "Sat Sri Akal" in the morning, Sat Sri Akal. I must go and pack.' Nooran hugged the old woman passionately. 'Sat Sri Akal,' she said a little breathlessly again and went out.

Jugga's mother sat on her charpoy staring into the dark for several hours.

Not many people slept in Mano Majra that night. They went from house to house—talking, crying, swearing love and friendship, assuring each other that this would soon be over. Life, they said, would be as it always had been.

Imam Baksh came back from his round of Muslim homes before Nooran had returned. Nothing had been packed. He was too depressed to be angry with her. It was as hard on the young as the old. She must have gone to see some of her friends. He started pottering around looking for gunny bags, tin canisters and trunks. A few minutes later Nooran came in.

'Have you seen all your girl friends? Let us get this done before we sleep,' said Imam Baksh.

'You go to bed. I will put the things in. There is not much to do—and you must be tired,' she answered.

'Yes, I am a little tired,' he said sitting down on his charpoy. 'You pack the clothes now. We can put in the cooking utensils in the morning after you have cooked something for the journey.' Imam Baksh stretched himself on the bed and fell asleep.

There was not much for Nooran to do. A Punjabi peasant's baggage consists of little besides a change of clothes, a quilt and a pillow, a couple of pitchers, cooking utensils, and perhaps a brass plate and a copper tumbler or two. All that can be put on the only piece of furniture they possess—a charpoy. Nooran put her own and her father's clothes in a gray battered steel trunk which had been with them ever since she could remember. She lit a fire in the hearth to bake a few chapatties for the next day. Within half an hour she had done the cooking. She rinsed the utensils and put them in a gunny bag. Flour, salt and the spices that remained went in biscuit and cigarette tins, which in their turn went inside an empty kerosene oil can with a wood top. The packing was over. All that remained was to roll her quilt round the pillow, put the odds and ends on the charpoy and the charpoy on the buffalo. She could carry the piece of broken mirror in her hand.

It rained intermittently all night. Early in the morning it became a regular downpour. Villagers who had stayed up most of the night fell asleep in the monotonous patter of rain and the opiate of the fresh morning breeze.

The tooting of motor horns and the high note of truck engines in low gear plowing their way through the slush and mud woke the entire village. The convoy went around Mano Majra looking for a lane wide enough to let their trucks in. In front was a jeep fitted with a loud-speaker. There were two officers in it—a Sikh (the one who had come after the ghost train) and a Muslim. Behind the jeep were a dozen trucks. One of the trucks was full of Pathan soldiers and another one full of Sikhs. They were all armed with sten guns.

The convoy came to a halt outside the village. Only the jeep could make its way through. It drove up to the center and stopped beside the platform under the peepul tree. The two officers stepped out. The Sikh asked one of the villagers to fetch the lambardar. The Muslim was joined by the Pathan soldiers. He sent them out in batches of three to knock at every door and ask the Muslims to come out. For a few minutes Mano Majra echoed to cries of 'All Muslims going to Pakistan come out at once. Come! All Muslims. Out at once.'

Slowly the Muslims began to come out of their homes, driving their cattle and their bullock carts loaded with charpoys, rolls of bedding, tin trunks, kerosene oil tins, earthen pitchers and brass utensils. The rest of Mano Majra came out to see them off.

The two officers and the lambardar were the last to come out of the village. The jeep followed them. They were talking and gesticulating animatedly. Most of the talking was between the Muslim officer and the lambardar.

'I have no arrangement to take all this luggage with bullock carts, beds, pots and pans. This convoy is not going to Pakistan by road. We are taking them to the Chundunnugger refugee camp and from there by train to Lahore. They can only take their clothes, bedding, cash and jewelry. Tell them to leave everything else here. You can look after it.'

The news that the Mano Majra Muslims were going to Pakistan came as a surprise. The lambardar had believed they would only go to the refugee camp for a few days and then return.

'No, Sahib, we cannot say anything,' replied the lambardar. 'If it was for a day or two we could look after their belongings. As you are going to Pakistan, it may be many months before they return. Property is a bad thing; it poisons people's minds. No, we will not touch anything. We will only look after their houses.'

The Muslim officer was irritated. 'I have no time to argue. You see yourself that all I have is a dozen trucks. I cannot put buffaloes and bullock carts in them.'

'No, Sahib,' retorted the lambardar stubbornly. 'You can say what you like and you can be angry with us, but we will not touch our brothers' properties. You want us to become enemies?'

'Wah, wah, Lambradar Sahib,' answered the Muslim laughing loudly. 'Shabash! Yesterday you wanted to kill them, today you call them brothers. You may change your mind again tomorrow.'

'Do not taunt us like this, Captain Sahib. We are brothers and will always remain brothers?'

'All right, all right, Lambardara. You are brothers,' the officer said. 'I grant you that, but I still cannot take all this stuff. You consult the Sardar Officer and your fellow villagers about it. I will deal with the Muslims.'

The Muslim officer got on the jeep and addressed the crowd. He chose his words carefully.

'We have a dozen trucks and all you people who are going to Pakistan must get on them in ten minutes. We have other villages to evacuate later on. The only luggage you can take with you is what you can carry—nothing more. You can leave your cattle, bullock carts, charpoys, pitchers, and so on with your friends in the village. If we get a chance, we will bring these things out for you later. I give you ten minutes to settle your affairs. Then the convoy will move.'

The Muslims left their bullock carts and thronged round the jeep, protesting and talking loudly. The Mulsim officer who had stepped off the jeep went back to the microphone.

'Silence! I warn you, the convoy will move in ten minutes; whether you are on it or not will be no concern of mine.'

Sikh peasants who had stood apart heard the order and went up to Sikh officer for advice. The officer took no notice of them; he continued staring contemptuously over the upturned collar of his raincoat at the men, cattle, carts and trucks steaming in the slush and rain.

'Why, Sardar Sahib,' asked Meet Singh nervously, 'is not the lambardar right? One should not touch another's property. There is always danger of misunderstanding.'

The officer looked Meet Singh up and down.

'You are quite right, Bhaiji, there is some danger of being misunderstood. One should never touch another's property; one should never look at another's woman. One should just let others take one's goods and sleep with one's sisters. The only way people like you will understand anything is by being sent over to Pakistan: have your sisters and mothers raped in front of you, have your clothes taken off, and be sent back with a kick and spit on on your behinds.'

The officer's speech was a slap in the face to all the peasants. But someone sniggered. Everyone turned around to look. It was Malli with his five companions. With them were a few young refugees who were staying at the Sikh temple. None of them belonged to Mano Majra.

'Sir, the people of this village are famous for their charity,' said Malli smiling. 'They cannot look after themselves, how can they look after other people? But do not bother, Sardar Sahib, we will take care of Muslim property. You can tell the other officer to leave it with us. It will be quite safe if you can detail some of your soldiers to prevent looting by these people.'

There was complete confusion. People ran hither and thither shouting at the tops of their voices. Despite the Muslim officer's tone of finality, villagers clamored around him protesting and full of suggestions. He came up to his Sikh colleague surrounded by his bewildered coreligionists.

'Can you make arrangements for taking over what is left behind?'

Before the Sikh could answer, a babel of protests burst from all sides. The Sikh remained tight-lipped and aloof.

The Muslim officer turned around sharply. 'Shut up!' he yelled.

The murmuring died down. He spoke again, punctuating each word with a stab of his forefinger.

'I give you five minutes to get into the trucks with just as much luggage as you can carry in your hands. Those who are not in will be left behind. And this is the last time I will say it.'

'It is all settled,' said the Sikh officer, speaking softly in Punjabi. 'I have arranged that these people from the next village will look after the cattle, carts, and houses till it is over. I will have a list made and sent over to you.'

His colleague did not reply. He had a sardonic smile on his face. Mano Majra Sikhs and Muslims looked on helplessly.

There was no time to make arrangements. There was no time even to say good-bye. Truck engines were started. Pathan soldiers rounded up the Muslims, drove them back to the carts for a brief minute, or two, and then onto the trucks. In the confusion of rain, mud and soldiers herding the peasants about with the muzzles of their sten guns sticking in their backs, the villagers saw little of each other. All they could do was to shout their last farewells from the trucks. The Muslim officer drove his jeep round the convoy to see that all was in order and then came to say good-bye to his Sikh colleague. The two shook hands mechanically, without a smile or a trace of emotion. The jeep took its place in front of the line of trucks. The microphone blared forth once more to announce that they were ready to move. The officer shouted 'Pakistan!' His soldiers answered in a chorus 'Forever!' The convoy slushed its way toward Chundunnugger. The Sikhs watched them till they were out of sight. They wiped the tears off their faces and turned back to their homes with heavy hearts.

Mano Majra's cup of sorrow was not yet full. The Sikh officer summoned the lambardar. All the villagers came with him—no one wanted to be left alone. Sikh soldiers threw a cordon round them. The officer told the villagers that he had decided to appoint Malli custodian of the evacuated Muslims' property. Anyone interfering with him or his men would be shot.

Malli's gang and the refugees then unyoked the bullocks, looetd the carts, and drove the cows and buffaloes away.

Karma

Sir Mohan Lal looked at himself in the mirror of a first-class waiting room at the railway station. The mirror was obviously made in India. The red oxide at its back had come off at several places and long lines of translucent glass cut across its surface.

Sir Mohan smiled at the mirror with an air of pity and patronage.

'You are so very much like everything else in this country, inefficient, dirty, indifferent,' he murmured.

The mirror smiled back at Sir Mohan.

'You are a bit of all right, old chap.' it said. 'Distinguished, efficient—even handsome. That neatly trimmed moustache—the suit from Saville Row with the carnation in the buttonhole—the aroma of eau de cologne, talcum powder, and scented soap all about you! Yes, old fellow, you are a bit of all right.'

Sir Mohan threw out his chest, smoothed his Balliol tie for the umpteenth time and waved a goodbye to the mirror.

He glanced at his watch. There was still time for a quick one.

'Koi Hai?'

A bearer in white livery appeared through a wire gauze door.

'Ek Chota,' ordered Sir Mohan, and sank into a large cane chair to drink and ruminate.

Outside the waiting room sir Mohan Lal's luggage lay piled along the wall. On a small grey steel trunk Lachmi, Lady Mohan Lal, sat chewing a betel leaf and fanning herself with a newspaper. She was short and fat and in her middle forties. She wore a dirty white sari with a red border. On one side of her nose glistened a diamond nose ring and she had several gold bangles on her arms. She had been talking to the bearer until Sir Mohan had summoned him inside. As soon as he had gone, she hailed a passing railway coolie.

'Where does the zenana stop?'

'Right at the end of the platform.'

The coolie flattened his turban to make a cushion, hoisted the steel trunk on his head, and moved down the platform. Lady Lal picked up her brass tiffin carrier and ambled along behind him. On the way she stopped by a hawker's stall to replenish her silver betel leaf case, and then joined the coolie. She sat down on her steel trunk (which the coolie had put down) and started talking to him.

'Are the trains very crowded on these lines?'

'These days all trains are crowded, but you'll find room in the zenana.'

'Then I might as well get over the bother of eating.'

Lady Lal opened the brass carrier and took out a bundle of cramped *chapaties* and some mango pickle. While she ate, the coolie sat opposite her on his haunches, drawing lines in the gravel with his finger.

'Are you traveling alone, sister ?'

'No, I am with my master, brother. He is in the waiting room. He travels first class. He is a vizier and a barrister, and meets so many officers and Englishmen in the trains—and I am only a native woman. I can't understand English and don't know their ways, so I keep to my zenana inter-class.'

Lachmi chatted away merrily. She was fond of a little gossip and had no one to talk to at home. Her husband never had any time to spare for her. She lived in the upper storey of the house and he on the ground floor. He did not like her poor illiterate relatives hanging about his bungalow, so they never came. He came up to her once in a while at night and stayed for a few minutes. He just ordered her about in anglicized Hindustani, and she obeyed passively. These nocturnal visits had, however, borne no fruit.

The signal came down and the clanging of the bell announced the approaching train. Lady Lal hurriedly finished off her meal. She got up, still licking the stone of the pickled mango. She emitted a long, loud belch as she went to the public tap to rinse her mouth and wash her hands. After washing she dried her mouth and hands with the loose end of her sari, and walked back to her steel trunk, belching and thanking the gods for the favor of a filling meal.

The train steamed in. Lachmi found herself facing an almost empty inter-class zenana compartment next to the guard's van, at the tail end of the train. The rest of the train was packed. She heaved her squat, bulky frame through the door and found a seat by the window. She produced a two-anna bit from a knot in her sari and dismissed the coolie. She then opened her betel case and made herself two betel leaves charged with a red and white paste, minced betelnuts and cardamoms. These she thrust into her mouth till her cheeks bulged on both sides. Then she rested her chin on her hands and sat gazing idly at the jostling crowd on the platform.

The arrival of the train did not disturb Sir Mohan Lal's sang-froid. He continued to sip his Scotch and ordered the bearer to tell him when he had moved the luggage to a firstclass compartment. Excitement, bustle, and hurry were exhibitions of bad breeding, and Sir Mohan was eminently well bred. He wanted everything 'tickety-boo' and orderly. In his five years abroad, Sir Mohan had acquired the manners and attitudes of the upper classes. He rarely spoke Hindustani. When he did, it was like an Englishman's—only the very necessary words and properly anglicized. But he fancied his English, finished and refined at no less a place than the University of Oxford. He was fond of conversation, and like a cultured Englishman he could talk on almost any subject—books, politics, people. How frequently had he heard English people say that he spoke like an Englishman!

Sir Mohan wondered if he would be travelling alone. It was a Cantonment and some English officers might be on the train. His heart warmed at the prospect of an impressive conversation. He never showed any sign of eagerness to talk to the English as most Indians did. Nor was he loud, aggressive, and opinionated like them. He went about his business with an expressionless matter-of-factness. He would retire to his corner by the window and get out a copy of *The Times*. He would fold it in a way in which the name of the paper was visible to others while he did the crossword puzzle. *The Times* always attracted attention. Someone would like to borrow it when he put it aside with a gesture signifying 'I've finished with it.' Perhaps someone would recognize his Balliol tie which he always wore while travelling. That would open a vista leading to a fairyland of Oxford colleges, masters, dons, tutors, boat races, and rugger matches. If both *The Times* and the tie failed, Sir Mohan would 'Koi Hai' his bearer to get the Scotch out. Whisky never failed with Englishmen. Then followed Sir Mohan's handsome gold cigarette case filled with English cigarettes. English cigarettes in India? How on earth did he get them? Sure he didn't mind? And Sir Mohan's understanding smile—of course he didn't. But could he use the Englishman as a medium to commune with his dear old England? Those five years of grey bags and gowns, of sports blazers and mixed doubles, of dinners at the Inns of Court and nights with Piccadilly prostitutes. Five years of a crowded glorious life. Worth far more than the forty-five in India with his dirty, vulgar countrymen, with sordid details of the road to success, of nocturnal visits to the upper storey and all-too-brief sexual acts with obese old Lachmi, smelling of sweat and raw onion.

Sir Mohan's thoughts were disturbed by the bearer announcing the installation of the Sahib's luggage in a firstclass coupe next to the engine. Sir Mohan walked to his coupe with a studied gait. He was dismayed. The compartment was empty. With a sigh he sat down in a corner and opened the copy of *The Times* he had read several times before.

Sir Mohan looked out of the window down the crowded platform. His face lit up as he saw two English soldiers trudging along, looking in all the compartments for room. They had their haversacks slung behind their backs and walked unsteadily. Sir Mohan decided to welcome them even though they were entitled to travel only second class. He would speak to the guard.

One of the soldiers came up to the last compartment and stuck his face through the window. He surveyed the compartment and noticed the unoccupied berth.

'Ere, Bill,' he shouted, 'one 'ere.'

His companion came up, also looked in, and looked at Sir Mohan.

'Get the nigger out,' he muttered to his companion.

They opened the door, and turned to the half-smiling, half-protesting Sir Mohan.

'Reserved!' yelled Bill.

'Janta—Reserved. Army—Fauj.' exclaimed Jim, pointing to his khaki shirt.

'Ek dum jao—get out!'

'I say. I say, surely,' protested Sir Mohan in his Oxford accent.

The soldiers paused. It almost sounded like English, but they knew better than to trust their inebriated ears. The engine whistled and the guard waved his green flag.

They picked up Sir Mohan's suitcase and flung it onto the platform. Then followed his Thermos-flask, suitcase, bedding and *The Times*. Sir Mohan was livid with rage.

'Preposterous, preposterous,' he shouted, hoarse with anger. 'I'll have you rrested—guard, guard!'

Bill and Jim paused again. It did sound like English, but it was too much of the King's for them.

'Keep yer ruddy mouth shut!' And Jim struck Sir Mohan flat on the face.

The engine gave another short whistle and the train began to move. The soldiers caught Sir Mohan by the arms and flung him out of the train. He reeled backwards, tripped on his bedding, and landed on the suitcase.

'Toodle-oo!'

Sir Mohan's feet were glued to the earth and he lost his speech. He stared at the lighted window of the train going past him in quickening tempo. The tail end of the train appeared with a red light and the guard standing, in the open doorway with the flags in his hands.

In the inter-class zenana compartment was Lachmi, fair and

and fat, on whose nose the diamond nose ring glistened against the station lights. Her mouth was bloated with betel saliva which she had been storing up to spit as soon as the train had cleared the station. As the train sped past the lighted part of the platform, Lady Lal spat and sent a jet of red dribble flying across like a dart.

(From *Black Jasmine*, Jaico 1977).

GLOSSARY

Alamgir: Protector
Arrere: Hey! A term of exclamation
Attar of roses: Perfume; scent of Roses
Babuji: A term of respect for a Hindu male
Bilayat: Mispronunciation of Vilayat, Hindi for England
Bahin chod: Sister fucker (a term of abuse)
Badshah: King
Betel leaf: Leaf of a plant which Indians wrap round bits of areca-nut and chew
Bulbul: Name of a bird
Betelnut: Areca-nut used in betel
Bhils: A primitive, local tribe
Bhai: Brother
Beybey: Bibi
Bibiji: A term of respect for a Hindu female
Brahmin: A member of the Hindu priestly class, highest in the Hindu caste hierarchy.
Budmash: Scoundrel
Chamar: Cobbler; a member of the scheduled caste
Chapattie: Small round of unleavened bread, baked on a griddle
Charpoy: Light bedstead with mattress of string
Chota babu: a term generally used for the younger male member in a Hindu family
Chacha: Paternal uncle
Dharam sastra: Hindu scriptures
Dada Maharaj: Great King
D.S.P.: Deputy Superintendent of Police
Ek chota: One small peg (of whisky or any alcohol)
Ek dum jao: Go away atonce
Elephant-god festival: Hindu festival surrounding the God Ganesh
Fauj: Army

Gayatri (Mantra): Brahmins' daily prayer
Gita: Short of *Bhagwadgita*, teachings of Lord Krishna
Ghee: Clarified butter
Gulabjaman: Indian Sweetmeat
Gurudwaras: Sikh temples
Har: Necklace
Harijan: A member of the scheduled caste
Hari-Om: Oh God Vishnu
Huzoor: Sir; term of respect
Izzat: Honour, reputation
Jai: Hail victory
Khabar: News
Khadi: Coarse cotton cloth, generally handwoven
Kikar tree: The tree *acacia*
Kisan: Farmer
Kuran: Muslim epic, Religious book of Muslims
Kamar: A blacksmith; a member of the scheduled caste
Kumkum: Red powder, used on the forehead by married Hindu women of India
Lakshmi: Hindu goddess of wealth
Lalaji: A term of respect used for a Hindu merchant
Lala: Merchant
Lathi: Long stick used by the police as weapon
Madar chod: Rape-mother (a term of abuse)
Maji: Term used for mother
Mahatma Gandhi Ki jai!: Victory to Mahatma Gandhi
Mai-bap: Mother-father
Mandal: Multitude, collection of people
Mufti: Plain clothes as opposed to uniform
Munshi: A learned man; a scribe
Namaste: Spoken greeting accompanying the act of joining palms in salutation
Nasib: Fate
Nazar: Ceremonial present
Octroi: Duty levied on goods entering town
Ohe: A term of exclamation, denoting grief, surprise, astonishment or lamentation
Pakoras: Fried dumplings
Paltans: Armed forces
Pan-dan: Box in which betel leaves are kept

Glossary

Pooja: Prayer
Praja-mandal: People's party
Pujari: Worshipper; priest
Purdah: Veil with which Indian women cover their faces
Puttee: Long strip of cloth wound spirally round leg from ankle to knee for protection and support
Rais: A title given to Indians during British rule
Rama: Hero of the epic Ramayana
Ramayana: Sanskrit epic describing the deeds of Lord Rama
Rasgula: Spongy sweetmeat ball
Sarkar: The state; government. The term is often loosely used to denote a man in authority
Satrenji: Multicoloured carpet
Seer: Indian weight denomination, approximating a kilo
Shaitan: Devil
Sivoham: Oh God Siva
Sat Sri Akal: Spoken greeting by Sardars
Sonar: Goldsmith
Shabash: Well done
Swamiji: A holy man
Tabala: Drum
Tehsildar: Native collector of revenue in *tehsil*—subdivision of a district in India
Thanedar: Police officer in charge of police station
Vande Matram: National song of India written by Bankim Chandra Chatterjee
Vay: A term denoting surprise, disgust
Vizier: High official, term often used for state minister
Yagna: Purification fire accompanied by prayers, an important ritual for the welfare of humanity
Zenana: Part of the house reserved for women in high-caste families